IDENTITY

I KNOW WHO I AM

Patrick Amadiegwu

IDENTITY: I KNOW WHO I AM

Copyright © 2022 Patrick Amadiegwu

All rights reserved. No part of this book may be reproduced or transmitted in any form or by any means without the written permission of the author.

Scriptures marked KJV are taken from the KING JAMES VERSION (KJV): KING JAMES VERSION, public domain.

Scripture taken from the New King James Version®. Copyright © 1982 by Thomas Nelson. Used by permission. All rights reserved.

Scripture quotations marked (NIV) are taken from the Holy Bible, New International Version®, NIV®. Copyright © 1973, 1978, 1984, 2011 by Biblica, Inc.™ Used by permission of Zondervan. All rights reserved worldwide. www.zondervan.com. The "NIV" and "New International Version" are trademarks registered in the United States Patent and Trademark Office by Biblica, Inc.™.

Scriptures marked AMP are taken from the AMPLIFIED BIBLE (AMP): Scripture taken from the AMPLIFIED® BIBLE, Copyright © 1954, 1958, 1962, 1964, 1965, 1987 by the Lockman Foundation Used by Permission. (www.Lockman.org)

Published by:
Eleviv Publishing Group
Centerville, OH 45458
info@elevivpublishing.com
www.elevivpublishing.com

ISBN: 978-1-952744-56-3 paperbook
       978-1-952744-57-0 ebook

Printed in the United States of America

Dedication

In honour and memory of my precious, irreplaceable, and gorgeous late mother, Patience Monica Amadiegwu alias Nwanyi Ghana.

APPRECIATION

I want to thank God Almighty, who inspired and motivated me to pen down this electrifying compendium through the auspices of His Holy Spirit. Special thanks to my wife, Ozioma Grace Amadiegwu. My special thanks to all my patron saints - Brother Cabi Fontenel & Family (Switzerland), Rev. Glenda Greutter De Leon (Co-founder @ Rhema Faith Embassy International Basel -Switzerland), Arnold & Zeni Montes (USA), Sister Sheneka Lockhart (Nikki) in the Bahamas, Dywight Baccus (Switzerland), Nico Schlasse (Germany), Bro. Fred Nwoke (Switzerland), A.J. Lukas Bahtosch (Switzerland), Sister Chinasa Nzeocha, Sister Phyllis Lovelace (London), and Mrs. Joy Ihejirika-Uwakwe.

ENDORSEMENTS

This book, **"IDENTITY- I KNOW WHO I AM,"** which I feel was inspired by God to benefit the reader, will encourage everyone who reads it through. Many people have missed their prophetic place due to things my friend, Pastor Patrick O. Amadiegwu, reveals in this book. Every person, I believe, has a prophetic destiny set by God, and it is up to us as individuals to seek that prophetic place that God has set for us. Pastor Patrick Amadiegwu's book releases the revelation I believe is needed for this time for the Church. To know one's identity and being "will require being sensitive to the voice and direction of God through the power of the Holy Spirit.

I look forward to seeing this great book published for others to experience what I have in this manuscript. May God bless you and the great work you do in the world for the Glory of God's Kingdom.

Global Peace Ambassador
Dr. Alwin Roland Timothy
Founder & International President Global Churches Alliance Ambassador At Large -International Human Rights Peace Commission U.S.A.

Pastor Patrick Amadiegwu is a dynamic and contemporary parcel of the virgin experience for everyone. For one already loaded in Spirit, it becomes an armament for positioning better with the cosmic and, for neophytes, an excellent gift for identification. A privilege to explore a right to ask yourself and answer the question, WHO AM I? Rediscover yourself, awaken God's deposits in you, and maximise your potential.

Professor George Chinedu Alozie
Department Of Architecture
Abia State University Uturu- Nigeria

God is God, and we are human beings. Every discourse on identity is an attempt to appreciate who God is and the complexities that go with creation. It illuminates the mind to unravel the mystery behind certain identities and crises. When such identities are undiscovered, the gravity of one's potential cannot be maximised. The journey of life can result in a complex construct if you are unaware of "Who You Are." God is a God of plan, purpose, design, and objectivity. He created humans as freelance beings to have a plan, purpose, design, and objectivity. God created human beings to recreate things, and this cannot be achieved when you are ignorant of your chemistry; hence the persistent question "Who Am I? lingers and needs to be individually answered. I strongly recommend this book, "IDENTITY-I KNOW WHO I AM," by Pastor Patrick Amadiegwu, to scholars, teachers, researchers, family, and the world.

Rt. Rev`D Dr. Bernard Nwaogu
Intervention Ministry – Onitsha, Nigeria.
Vice President, New Day Ministerial Association.
Lecturer, New Dimension Seminaries, Lagos, Nigeria.

In the social jungle of human experience, from the workplace to family relationships, there can be a push for us to match the personalities and identities of those around us. This book, "IDENTITY-I KNOW WHO I AM," will help you explore your true identity and live meaningfully daily.

Bishop Abel Kungu Snr.
Presiding Bishop, Acts of Faith Ministries International,
Bedford -England.

Table of Contents

Dedication
Appreciation
Endorsement

01. IDENTITY 10
02. EMOTIONAL INTELLIGENCE/CHRISTIAN PERSPECTIVE 32
03. LIVING YOUR IDENTITY 44
04. THE BOUNCE-BACK MENTALITY 47
05. THE TRICHOTOMY OF HUMAN BEINGS 55
06. PERSONIFIED IDENTITY 65
07. SELF-ESTEEM BECOMES YOUR VALUE 74
08. COGNITIVE BEHAVIOR/ FAITH 83
09. THE WINNER'S BRAIN 91
10. SELF-CONSCIOUSNESS 96
11. SPLIT THE SEA SO I CAN WALK ON 101
12. DIVINE POWER/ AUTHORITY IS A LOGICAL CONSTRUCT 106
13. WHAT YOU SPEAK LOCATES WHO YOU ARE 120
14. APPLYING THE LAW OF GRAVITY AND AERODYNAMICS IN THE SUPERNATURAL 130

15. LONELINESS IS NOT ALONENESS *135*
16. TRANSFORMATION IS INTERNAL *145*
17. UNDERSTANDING DIVINE PROGRESSION *150*
18. WHO IS SAINT? *159*
19. LIVING THE VOLUME OF WHAT IS WRITTEN *168*
20. CALLED TO BE AMBASSADORS *173*
21. PERSONIFIED INDIVIDUAL *187*
22. THE CHARACTER OF YOUR THOUGHTS *198*
23. MANIFESTING THE ABILITY OF GOD
    WITHIN YOU *207*
24. THE GARDEN OF EDEN IN YOUR HEART *253*
25. INCARNATION OF MAN *261*
26. SMALL THINGS THAT MAKE YOU LOSE
    GOD'S BIG *266*
27. WISDOM IN YOUR DESTINY *276*
28. PHYSICAL BUT LIVING IN THE
    SUPERNATURAL *282*
29. CONFESSION IS THE LOCATION OF
    YOUR DESTINY *288*
30. A POSSESSOR OF LEGAL VICTORY *299*
31. THE CONSCIOUSNESS OF THE ENERGY
    IN YOU *305*

CHAPTER 1

IDENTITY
(I KNOW WHO I AM)

The word identity comes from a middle French word, identite -the quality of being the same, sameness and from Latin, identitas -the quality of being the same, the condition or fact that an entity is itself and nothing else; identitas is the quality of being the same, the condition or fact that an entity is itself and not another thing.

Identity is a fact of being who or what a person or thing is. The qualities, beliefs, personality, appearance, and expressions make a person or group. A psychological identity relates to self-image, self-esteem, and individuality. It is who you are, how you think about yourself, your perceptions and the way the world around you perceives you, and the characteristics that define you. It is a name or persona- the mask or appearance one presents to the world by which one is known. Identity is the difference or character that masks off an individual from the rest of the same kind, selfhood. Identity connotes cultural identity, professional identity, ethnic and national identity, religious identity, gender, and disability identity; all of these influence who you are.

Identity is a journey of self-discovery. It's not found in your name, beauty, degree, vocabulary, position, possession, accolades, family tree, inheritance, etc. Identity is not a definition. If you cannot see your identity, you cannot see your ability and will also not operate in the gravity of your potential. When you know who you are, you have power. When you know your identity, you have the authority and authenticity to operate and function in your capacity anywhere, any place, and under any circumstance.

Power without authority makes one enfeeble. Authority makes power meaningful. Who are you? Many people cannot be themselves because they cannot find themselves. They seek refuge in something lesser than them because they cannot find who they are.

There are divinely ordained expectations for every human being on earth. There is a purpose why God brought you into the world. You are not a happenstance. God's Word always has didactical intent. God is a God of progress; everything in our lives should be moving forward and not depreciating.

You can break the paralysis of being unidentified by possessing a highly evolved sense of self-awareness. When you narrow the gap between your public and authentic self, it is easier to read how others experience you. Your attitude is a product of belief. Your attitude comes from your belief system. Heights always mean leverage, the height of your connections, your influence, and your ideas and creativity; they all converge to elevate you to airspace where others can't compete. Don't allow your fear to be greater than your purpose.

The pinnacle of your truth is that which leads you to a place of sovereignty—a place where any circumstances cannot move you. You have a fixed position because of the authority of God's Word. The light in you will not shine if you are extinguished. If you don't freeze your tail off, you might not attain genuine success. Build your vision from the ground and discover yourself. Knowledge should become as familiar to us and as usable as the multiplication table. Someone must pioneer it and begin to teach it.

The intent is the most critical component of motivation. It is the source of inspiration and why you can create something. The intent is usually hidden; understanding your intent gives you the "big picture" of your purpose. God has put a purpose for everything He does. The revelation of your identity creates purpose; the revelation allows you to escape damnation. The only thing you need to achieve significance is to be intentional about your starting; no matter where you are, who you are, or what you have, you can't make an impact sitting still. The purpose of life is not only to be happy but to be successful and valuable. *"But it is the spirit in a person, the breath of the Almighty, that gives them understanding." Job 32:8 (NIV)*

God has expressed himself in you. He has voice printed you; your DNA has been voice printed. You must express yourself in the world, your region, your environment, your crisis, and your troubles; you need to express yourself. You are designed to operate in dominion, and you cannot settle for the little when you have access to the colossal. You are a spiritual and mental magnet attracting to yourself all things which bless and prosper you. The great things of life are simple, dynamic, and creative, and you are that mechanism. God is a God of plan, purpose, design, and objectivity. Before entering the earthly realm, God has already masterminded a plan for your life; you are the one to harness what God planned for your life.

Man is a spirit; he has a soul and lives in a body, but the reality is that man is a soul. *"And the Lord God formed man of the dust of the ground, and breathed into his nostrils the breath of life; and man became a living soul." Genesis 2:7 (KJV)*

You cannot define yourself based on the physical body. One of the most vital parts of who you are is your soul; if you fail to nourish your soul, then you have failed to nourish yourself and your emotion. God gives you prudence through His word to go through life circumstances and definitions. Your mind is the sea and chronicle of all conflicts. What controls your mind controls your life and shifts your thought-life. You cannot change the world until you change yourself.

You are not powerful until you empower yourself and somebody else. Maturity is a product of your process, not your giftedness or anointing. Gold can't be gold until it passes through the processing of fire. For every new season of your life, a new level of revelation is required, but be assured that if you survived the process, God has the provision. *"Therefore when Jesus perceived that they were about to come and take Him by force to make Him king, He departed again to the mountain by Himself alone." John 6:15 (NKJV)*

The breath of life that made you a living soul gives you the ability of perceptivity. The soul of man is capable of perceiving; it is sensitive to occurrences, discerning in nature, and observant.

The soul of man is a substance that can be wasted, like the case of the lost son in Luke 15, who did not waste only his substance but wasted his soul before he became conscious of who he was, whose son he was, and therefore able to come to knowledge. *"And not many days after, the younger son gathered all together, journeyed to a far country and there wasted his possession with prodigal living." Luke 15:13 (NKJV)* Loneliness is not the absence of people but the absence of purpose. When you find meaning, the people will come, but when you waste your purpose in life, you become desolate. Most times, people define you based on your outward manifestation, but the people in question do not know who you are. Relationships are born to define you, make you happy, feel you are wanted and cherished, or belittle you. *Jesus withdrew Himself from the people who do not know Him (John 6:15).* Your soul is responsible for your identity. If the enemy can control your soul, He can control your identity; external forces will govern your life and circumstances. If you refuse to make some "I –Statements," you will live your life with" "You-Statements," and "you-statements" are what people say about you, their tags, and your definition of yourself. You begin to live a life that is remote-controlled, tagged, and defined by external forces.

When you are rejected because of your "I-Statements" (I know who I am, I am in charge, I exercise dominion), that is not a sign that something is wrong with you. Rejection is a divine announcement that the person who rejected you no longer has the capacity for your greatness because you are impregnated with divine purposes that no human has control over. *For "who has known the mind of the LORD that he may instruct Him?" But we have the mind of Christ. 1 Corinthians 2:16 (NKJV)*

Our God is an economist. He does not waste any experience, so you are designed and fashioned not to destroy your spiritual and divine experiences. Stop looking for the definition people give you; it will not make you comfortable and carries some complexes. Stop asking the permission of people to be just who you are. Getting back at your enemy means you have to crave to be successful and purpose-oriented. Have a positive mind like Christ because you are Christ-like.

The problem is that your environment has picked up so many mental viruses, lies, and stereotypes about you that are contrary to God's vision. You need to come in the volume of what is written, "God's revelation of you." *Matthew 4:7(KJV) "Jesus said unto him (devil), it is written again, Thou shall not tempt the Lord thy God."* Jesus is very conscious of His identity, and He comes in the volume of what is written of Him. It is apparent you cannot live an abundant life ignorant of who you are and what is written of you.

Every problem is a test of your potential. God moves through crisis in your life. Crisis is a divine announcement that God is ready for the outpouring of your abundance and wants you to move to a higher level. Every crisis will want to question your identity; who are you? The discovery of who you are will determine how you come out of your fire.

People who are a product of their environment are lacking in identity. Your calling is a calling to rule from everywhere, even in desert and dry grounds.

Then God said, "Let Us make man in Our image, according to Our likeness; let them have dominion over the fish of the sea, over the birds of the air, and over the cattle, over all the earth and over every creeping thing that creeps on the earth." Genesis 1:26 (NKJV)

You are created in the Image means you have dominion, and

to have dominion means operating in higher frequencies. God gave you the capability to function on higher frequencies to subdue and exercise dominion consistently; you cannot do this if you don't know who you are.

When your identity is in crisis, you then have a low frequency, and that is when you make such confessions that are not written of you like: I am sick, I have depression, I am weak and poor, I don't have luck, I think I am under a demonic influence, I am jobless-all these are as a result of low frequency, and a loss of identity. The devil takes advantage, knowing you have lost who you are.

God reveals Himself to you at the speed of thought, and the devil also reveals himself and seduces you at the speed of thought. Change your frequencies to higher frequencies of thought. *"Awake, awake, Deborah! Awake, awake, sing a song! Arise, Barak, and lead your captives away, O son of Abinoam! Judges 5:12 (NKJV)*

You might be the prophetic Deborah or Barak. God wants you to operate in higher frequencies to overcome your captives; everything that opposes the will of God for your life is a captive. Awakening means you are conscious on one level, but there is a calling to move to a higher level. You cannot afford to remain in the earthly room, but you must move to the throne room and pick up some divine conversation and announcement.

When you are so much in the flesh, you become sensitive to the things of the five senses, but when you move in higher frequencies, the Holy Spirit becomes your throne room transmitter. The Holy Spirit is a prophetic Spirit; He gets you impregnated with heavenly conversations and revelations and is always waiting to hear from the throne room to communicate. God is restoring dignity to restore expression. *And He Himself gave some to be apostles, some prophets, some evangelists and some pastors and teachers for the equipping of the saints for the work of ministry, for the edifying of the body of Christ. Ephesians 4:11-12(NKJV)*

Christians are called to work not to complicate but to complete one another. The moon does not compete with the sun; it completes the sun. Anytime you want to build muscles, you need some resistance. God is releasing new mantels and anointing that will cause you to break laws that break barriers. You cannot do exploits on earth by living the breath of life in you on low frequencies because there is a diabolical model for every kingdom model. As you rise to higher frequencies, there will always be diabolical confrontations, and living the breath of life in you propels you through. Your blessings are in the breaking. Your feet will never take you where your mind has never been.

It is impossible for a child of God to be a happenstance. You cannot have the breath of life, **("And the Lord God formed man of the dust of the ground and breathed into his nostrils the breath of life; and man became a living soul" Genesis 2:7**

KJV) and be a happenstance. You are designed for dominion, to subdue and rule over situations and circumstances. You are created to make an impact; hence, to exist is out of your vocabulary. There is a difference between having the anointing of God and God's mantel. The anointing gives you the power to function, but the mantel gives you authority and dominion to rule over realms, regions, and spheres. You are invested with abilities to defy every demographic barrier and onslaughts set before you. Anointing and mantel have no gender specifics or limitations. Elijah and Deborah are examples of the mantels, the kind of anointing that puts you out of emotional blackmail. When you lack the anointing of God or His mantel, you don't reign in the realm of the dominion because your frequencies and electric currents are too low. When your frequencies are low, your mind can be infected with viruses. You begin to take counsel from the devilish spirits, and that is when you start to make wrong confessions like "I am frustrated, I am a failure, depressed and have no future, God does not heal me and does not hear my prayer, I am sick and tired," etc. This is when you know you need the anti-virus to clean your mind, God's word. The viruses have their higher level, so you need to operate in higher frequencies to clean up and destroy some viruses in your mind. *And do not be conformed to this world, but be transformed by the renewing of your mind, that you may prove what is that good and acceptable and perfect will of God. Romans 12:2 (NKJV)*

Warfare is the counselling of the human mind by the Spirit of God. When you are elevated in the Spirit of God, you are operating in a higher frequency and realm of dominion. *Psalms 137:4 (KJV) How shall we sing the LORD'S song in a strange land?* If there is any place to sing the Lord's song, it is in a strange land, in your crisis. Every problem, trial, mountain, desert place, and valley are strange lands. You cannot sing the Lord's song in a strange land unless you operate in a higher frequency or put on a higher anointing and mantel of God. *Acts 16:25* tells us that Paul and Silas in their strange land prayed and sang and the Holy Ghost came down.

But at midnight Paul and Silas were praying and singing hymns to God and the prisoners were listening to them. Suddenly there was a great earthquake, so that the foundations of the prison were shaken; and immediately all the doors were opened and everyone's chains were loosed. Acts 16:25-26 (NKJV) When operating in a higher frequency, you can sing the Lord's song in the avalanche of troubles, in every situation, every crisis. Singing the Lord's song in a strange land puts the Holy Spirit to work. The Lord's song enables the Holy Spirit to penetrate your closed doors and begins to open them to you, loose you, and set you free from your captives. *"Therefore if the Son makes you free, you shall be free indeed." John 8:36 (NKJV)*

When you pray the problem, you exaggerate the situation. Pray the promise, don't pray the situation. In the middle of an identity crisis, we are surrounded by people who don't know where we are going and hence are no solution. In your identity crisis, find your Jonathan as David did. Your Jonathan will join you in prayers and counselling.

If money is your crisis, you must have your agenda, what the future will look like, and have a plan of the future you want; if life is a game, know the rules. If you tell your story for pity, you undermine your prosperity and progress. Tell your story so that you can get principles. It takes too much energy to be someone else. So be who you are. Discover your identity and lay hold on the volume of what is written of you. Refuse to allow someone's insecurity to be projected on you. Someone's insecurity is not an indication of your insecurity. The problem is that we often turn around to people who have never been where we want to go. You don't go to church or God for emotionalism but to learn the pitch. It is not what people are saying about you but what you are saying about yourself. People reflect who you are when you change after discovering your identity. When you discover your identity, things change for good; you begin to operate at a higher level because you are conscious of who you are.

Do not place your feet on sinking sand even when it seems you are losing your mind. Don't nurse your predicament and pains but transform them into miracles. Your dilemma is not eternal; the only thing that lasts forever is an intimate relationship with God. God's Word is the constructor of life. It changes any contrary information that is against your destiny. One can grow wise, but if that wisdom is without God, that one grows corrupt. Distraction is the destruction of your dreams and purpose in slow motion. Forget what you don't have and use what you have to come into divine alignment.

A Christian life without the passion for Christ and consciousness is living an ordinary human life and going through the same thing a natural or carnal man goes through. Sometimes people may not and will not recognize you, but it does not stop your divine paradigm shift. What God wants you to do is transcend the biological concerns with the survival of the self to experience the supernatural. God has predestined our existence to operate like a farmer planting seed in a field. God walks through the agricultural principle of planting a seed and reaping a harvest. Your small beginning can become mighty. God wants you to be -positive-minded because you are pregnant with destiny. Your knowledge must grow beyond your condition. Your blessing is not tied to anyone's opinion. Don't ever take a solo flight into your God-given destiny; you will eventually lose momentum, no matter how talented or gifted you feel you are.

The word of God in your mouth is God –talking. When you come in the volume of what is written of you in the scriptures, you are exercising dominion. The word of God you speak moves molecules (causes chemical reactions), and molecules have memories that go from a train track into the realm of the Spirit and come back to you as an experience.

1 Corinthians 2:9-16 (NKJV) But as it is written: "Eye has not seen, nor ear heard, Nor have entered into the heart of man The things which God has prepared for those who love Him."

But God has revealed them to us through His Spirit. For the Spirit searches all things, yes, the deep things of God. For what man knows the things of a man except the spirit of the man which is in him? Even so no one knows the things of God except the Spirit of God. Now we have received, not the Spirit of the world but the Spirit who is from God, that we might know the things that have been freely given to us by God. These things we also speak, not in words which man's wisdom teaches but which the Holy Spirit teaches, comparing spiritual things with spiritual. But the natural man does not receive the things of the Spirit of God, for they are foolishness to him; nor can he know them, because they are spiritually discerned. But he who is spiritual judges all things, yet he himself is rightly judged by no one. For "who has known the mind of the Lord that he may instruct Him?" But we have the mind of Christ.

Appropriate all things God has made available for you and watch your life grow in unending success and prosperity. You are the character of your thought. The character of your words and the totality of your personality are an expression of your thought chemistry.

Keep your heart with all diligence, For out of it spring the issues of life. Proverbs 4.23 (NKJV) **What the world advertises** to you are lies; they are full of deception and stereotypes. There are Christians who became born again after a year and have already become spiritual giants, and there are some who have been born again for 20 years in the church but are still babies and still wearing spiritual diapers.

Thoughts are more than imaginations; they are mental theatres with constructive or destructive abilities. Thoughts have the power to keep you enslaved or liberate you to be the best of a kind. Your life and circumstances will not change until you change your thinking. A man is not recreated by his belief but by his confession of the Lordship of Jesus. The reason is that righteousness of faith does not only believe but speak.

Job 22:28-29 You shall also decree a thing and it shall be established unto thee; and the light shall shine upon thy ways when men are cast down, then thou shall say, There is lifting up, and He shall save the humble person.

Revelation 12:11 (KJV) And they overcame him by the blood of the Lamb and by the word of their testimony; and they loved not their lives unto the death.

The word of God in your mouth creates tensions, which are so powerful that they impact your life. You open yourself to divine intervention and inspiration when your frequency is high. New revelation begins to pour out and supersaturate you. The frequency is a catalyst that propels you to pick revelation from God's throne room.

Your eyes are too pure to look on evil; you cannot tolerate wrongdoing. Why then do you tolerate the treacherous? Why are you silent while the wicked swallow up those more righteous than themselves? Habakkuk 1:13(NIV)

Every human being is a magnet with the potential to attract and repel Anyone with sorrow always around them repels God's presence in them. Sorrow is a choice; to be joyful is another; your system is designed not to harbor sorrow. It is not the things that happen to you that hurt you but how you respond to the things that happened to you. You will not know the secret of success until you know how to handle failure. Wisdom knows how and when to ignore. There is a difference between failure as a person and failure of an event. That your event failed does not make you a failure.

Psalm 139:14 &17-18 (NIV) I praise you because I am fearfully and wonderfully made; your works are wonderful, I know that full well. How precious to me are your thoughts, God! How vast is the sum of them! Were I to count them, they would outnumber the grains of sand— when I awake, I am still with you.

God's perception of you should be allowed to dwell in your subconsciousness. Refuse to accept demeaning or defaming thoughts, descriptions, or perceptions of your personality. You are God's excellent handiwork and perfect creation; that's how God mirrors you- *"For we are God's (own) handiwork (His workmanship) Ephesians 2:10.*

Never appraise or use men's negative descriptions and opinions to evaluate yourself; what matters is how God sees you in a light that no other person can. God created a manual which is His word that mirrors all your glorious features and inherent abilities. All you need do is to keep looking into the mirror of God.

James 1:25 (NKJV) says, "But he looks into the perfect law of liberty and continues in it and is not a forgetful hearer but a doer of the work, this one will be blessed in what he does.

God issued to you an extraordinary life and identity that no demographic onslaughts can change. Still, all you need do is self-discover yourself, "Who are you? Discover the gifting and supernatural abilities of God deposited in you. Apostle Paul instructs Christians in *2 Timothy 1:6 to "stir up the gift of God, which is in you."* Be conscious of your uniqueness; you are not an accident or needy seeking help; God already favored you. You are not a beggar but a child of the Most High God and are not at the mercy of anyone but the mercy of God.

The Holy Spirit lives in you, and the Scripture declares that all things are yours. *Therefore let no one boast in men. For all things are yours: whether Paul or Apollos or Cephas or the world or life or death, or things present or things to come- all are yours. 1 Corinthians 3:21-22(NKJV)*

2 Peter 1:3-5 says, "as His divine power has given to us all things that pertain to life and godliness, through the knowledge of Him who called us by glory and virtue, by which have been given to us exceedingly great and precious promises, that through these you may be partakers of divine nature, having escaped the corruption that is in the world through lust. But also for this very reason, giving all diligence, add to your faith virtue, to virtue knowledge,"

The fact that you are more than a conqueror and a victor in Christ Jesus, superior to Satan and the cohorts of darkness, is enough to make you express your gratitude to God. Learn to rejoice over the Word of God and celebrate its efficacy and power in your life. Celebrate God rather than celebrate crisis and problems. *Psalms 16:6 (NKJV) The lines have fallen to me in pleasant places; Yes, I have a good inheritance.*

This affirmative declaration implies that the property has been apportioned, but your portion has a treasure in it. God has given you a goodly heritage, an incredible inheritance. Child of God, an extraordinary inheritance has been delivered to you; you have been brought into a prominent place of irreversible dominion, destiny, success, and identity. You need to learn more and act more to express your heritage. Your inheritance is in Christ Jesus; just as you cannot discover your oil, gold, or diamond on the surface, except if you dig deeper into the earth, you must dig deep into the word of God to discover your identity and treasures of your inheritance in Christ and appropriate them to your life. Discover who you are so you can carry out the purpose why you are planted here on earth.

For in him we live, and move, and have our being; as certain also of your own poets have said, For we are also his offspring. Acts 17:28 (KJV)

God is a success and He reproduces after His kind. *1 Peter 1:23 (KJV) says, Being born again, not of corruptible seed, but of incorruptible, by the word of God, which liveth and abideth for ever.*

God gave birth to you, and you are His offspring. He does not want any failure or damage associated with you. You have His life and nature of righteousness because you are born of the word and Spirit of the Lord. You are on a predestined journey of success, prosperity, and health.

1 John 4:4 &17 (NIV) says, "You, dear children, are from God and have overcome them, because the one who is in you is greater than the one who is in the world. vs17. This is how love is made complete among us so that we will have confidence on the day of judgment: In this world we are like Jesus.

You inherited the attributes of Jesus Christ, the same dominion, and abilities He demonstrated on earth. You choose to express your dominion by supersaturating yourself with the consciousness of who you have been created for. You are not an accident here on earth, and you are not a happenstance; you cannot just happen; you are planted here on earth for a purpose. God created the universe, and you have a portion on which you are appointed to exercise dominion. You are not here only for gains; your identity also calls for exploitation.

Daniel 11:32 (KJV) And such as do wickedly against the covenant shall he corrupt by flatteries: but the people that do know their God shall be strong, and do exploits.

Therefore, manifest success everywhere you go and win every day in your life. The Psalmist defines the life of success and productivity God has made available for us. *And he shall be like a tree planted by the rivers of water, that bringeth forth his fruit in his season; his leaf also shall not wither; and whatsoever he doeth shall prosper. Psalm 1:3 (KJV)*

It may be that your life experiences have been in contrast with these realities, the realities of an overcomer.

1 John 5:4 (NKJV) For whatever is born of God overcomes the world. And this is the victory that has overcome the world- our faith.

However, it cannot invalidate the truth that you are God's offspring and a progeny of success. You are created in the likeness and image of God to express beauty, glory, and prosperity in every endeavor. Therefore, refuse to struggle. The struggle is not expressed in your identity. *Philippians 4:13 "I can do all things through Christ who strengthens me."*

You have the inherent "Dunamis," the dynamic ability to

cause changes. You have received supernatural power for effectiveness and efficiency. When you receive the Holy Ghost, He propels you to your higher frequencies, and you begin to destroy every demographic onslaught of the enemy. Never zero-point your human weakness, limitations, or physical abilities; look inwardly to the Holy Spirit for your empowerment and enablement.

Discover your identity, express your identity, and become a mighty instrument in the hand of God. Extraordinary people do extraordinary things. God is looking for identity-conscious Christians to express His supernatural nature on earth, efficacious and efficient ministers of the Gospel. They exhibit extraordinary enablement they received from the Holy Ghost.

God has made you a prophet of your life and the lives of others. You are the mouthpiece of God. The mouth is the compass of your life that propels your destiny. Words are powerful; they constitute the building blocks of your life. Whether you know it or not, you built whatever life you are living right now with your words. If you are dissatisfied with your present circumstance, you can take charge and change and steer your life to a new course through words.

Acts 20:32 (NKJV) So now, brethren, I commend you to God and to the word of His grace, which is able to build you up and give you an inheritance among all those who are sanctified.

Your primary assignment in life is to do the work of the ministry. This is your highest calling; every other thing is secondary. You may be a governor, lawyer, medical doctor, politician, etc., but leading men and women into righteousness is your primary responsibility here on earth. You may say you are not a pastor or evangelist; God's work is not only for these two but also for God's saints, including you.

Ecclesiastes 12:13 Let us hear the conclusion of the whole matter, fear God and keep His commandment, For this is man's all.

Ephesians 4:11-12 And He gave some, apostles, and some prophets; and some, evangelists and some pastors and teachers; For the perfecting of the saints, for the work of the ministry, for the edifying of the body of Christ.

The work of the ministry is the reconciliation of the world to God. You have a divine mandate to turn men and women from darkness to light and from the power of Satan unto God. God is preached under the anointing of the Spirit; it ministers grace to your spirit and impacts your mind and soul. God communicates with your spirit; you can only relate to him from your spirit, not your mind or physical body. The reason is that you are a spirit being as a human. That's why a man may still have all his faculties intact when he dies, but it remains lifeless. This is because the real person, the spirit, has left the body.

CHAPTER 2

EMOTIONAL INTELLIGENCE/ CHRISTIAN PERSPECTIVE

Emotional intelligence is the capacity to be aware of control, express one's emotions, and manage interpersonal relationships judiciously and empathetically. Emotional Intelligence quotient is the ability of individuals to recognise their own emotions and those of others, discern between different feelings and label them appropriately by using emotional information to guide thinking and behavior, and manage and adjust emotions to adapt to environments or towards achieving one goal.

Having IQ (Intelligent quotient) is an advantage, but having Emotional Intelligence can make all the difference to your future. Emotional intelligence determines our ability to manage our feelings and relationships. An emotional intelligence matrix means straddling your fence and evolving or developing. One must have the capacity to be self-wired and self-assessed.

Genesis 1:27 (NIV)So God created mankind in his own image, in the image of God he created them; male and female he created them.

Emotional Intelligence and the Christian perspective are compatible if we consider the fruit of the Spirit. Where man is weak, God can show Himself strong rather than believers making changes from human strength; they should lean on the power of the Holy Spirit. Some virtues are critical to maintaining a high emotional intelligence quotient, Self-awareness, empathy & social awareness, self-management, and social skills and relationships.

Many Scriptures vividly support self-awareness, positive psychology (optimism), (forgiveness, and mercy) and self-management, empathy, compassion, service, social awareness, and relationship. Throughout the old testament, many examples of God and emotional stories, characters and humans reveal deep feelings.

By improving your EQ (emotional intelligence) and taking active steps to make changes, you will find you are more productive and can build productive relationships. Emotional intelligence is vital, intrinsic, or essential to who you are and impacts every facet of our lives. Emotional Intelligence encompasses self-awareness, self-management, self-motivation, self-regulation, which is the ability to control your emotions and responses, Empathy and Relational, which help you understand and feel for others, their emotions, build and maintain relationships and manage conflicts.

EQ (Emotional Quotient) isn't the enemy of IQ (Intelligence Quotient). It is possible to have high levels of both. However, life is an inherently social construct; without the ability to function well within this relational environment, it is doubtful how far intelligence alone will get you or make you successful.

Self-awareness as a believer- *Philippians 4:13 "I can do all things through Christ who strengthens me." (NKJV)*

Colossians 1:9 (NKJV) (Preeminence of Christ) "For this reason, we also, since the day we heard it, do not cease to pray for you, and to ask that you may be filled with the knowledge of His will in all wisdom and spiritual understanding; "

Empathy & Social awareness- *Mark 12:31(NKJV) "You shall love your neighbour as yourself. There is no other commandment greater than these."*

Proverbs 18:2 A fool has no delight in understanding, But in expressing his own heart. (NKJV).

Self-management- *Galatians 5:22 But the fruit of the Spirit is love, joy, peace, long-suffering, kindness, goodness, faithfulness, (NKJV)*

Proverbs 17:22 A merry heart [a]does good, like medicine, But a broken spirit dries the bones." (NKJV)

Philippians 4:6-7 "Be anxious for nothing, but in everything by prayer and supplication, with thanksgiving, let your requests be made known to God; and the peace of God, which surpasses all understanding, will guard your hearts and minds through Christ Jesus." (NKJV)

Social skills and relationships- *Matthew 5:9 "Blessed are the peacemakers, For they shall be called sons of God." (NKJV)*

Mark 10:45 "For even the Son of Man did not come to be served, but to serve, and to give His life a ransom for many." (NKJV)

Proverbs 22:24 "Make no friendship with an angry man, And with a furious man do not go," (NKJV)

Proverbs 15:28 "The heart of the righteous studies how to answer, But the mouth of the wicked pours forth evil." (NKJV)

In the New Testament, Christ displays emotions through His communication and action. The Apostles stories included expanded connection to feelings and show that they have a significant, meaningful place in the believers life. Self-awareness and personal understanding allow application, expansion, and focus. As feelings are understood, they take their place in the spiritual life of faith.

Proverbs 4:7-8 Wisdom is the principal thing; Therefore get wisdom. And in all your getting, get understanding. Exalt her, and she will promote you; She will bring you honor, when you embrace her. (NKJV)

The emotional intelligence matrix of a Christian includes the fact that God's truth is all truth. A Christian should have a predisposition or tendency to see, plan and purpose in life, see the Creator in the creations, and have a spirit-guided life.

Romans 8:14 says, " For as many as are led by the Spirit of God, these are sons of God."

A Christian should be able to live with hope, optimism, and positive psychology, knowing that God is in control, God has a plan for a believer, and a believer should be assertive.

- *Jeremiah 29:11 For I know the thoughts that I think toward you, says the Lord; thoughts of peace and not of evil, to give you a future and a hope. (NKJV)*

Experience empathy and understanding- love one another, live with compassion and compassion should be the passion of a believer, have benevolence-be giving and kind or philanthropic.

1 Corinthians 13:1-4&13 Though I speak with the tongues of men and of angels, but have not love, I have become sounding brass or a clanging cymbal. And though I have the gift of prophecy, and understand all mysteries and all knowledge, and though I have all faith, so that I could remove mountains, but have not love, I am nothing. And though I bestow all my goods to feed the poor, and though I give my body [a]to be burned, but have not love, it profits me nothing. Love suffers long and is kind; love does not envy; love does not parade itself, is not [b]puffed up; And now abide faith, hope, love, these three; but the greatest of these is love. (NKJV)

Be a Resilient Christian- having the capacity to recover quickly from difficulties, toughness, and knock-downs like we often see in boxers. It is the ability of substance to spring back into shape, elasticity, and abrasion resistance. Renew, refresh and recover quickly. Setbacks provide learning and experiences. God is still Lord amid all setbacks, confrontations, and persecutions.

Isaiah 43:2 When you pass through the waters, I will be with you; And through the rivers, they shall not overflow you. When you walk through the fire, you shall not be burned, Nor shall the flame scorch you. (NKJV)

Meditate on God's Word, and pray without ceasing. PUSH means to pray until something happens. PRAY is praise, repent, ask, yield, expect and rejoice. Be Christ-like, have the attitude of Christ and fruits of the Spirit.

1 John 4:17(NKJV) Love has been perfected among us in this: that we may have boldness in the day of judgment; because as He is, so are we in this world.

John 1:16 (NKJV) And of His fullness we have all received, and grace for grace.

John 14:12 (NKJV) Most assuredly, I say to you, he who believes in Me, the works that I do he will do also; and greater works than these he will do, because I go to My Father.

We as believers should have matured, supportive communication, conversations, and relationships and be quick to forgive.

2 Peter 3:18 (NIV) but grow in the grace and knowledge of our Lord and Saviour Jesus Christ. To Him be the glory both now and forever. Amen.

Colossians 4:6 Let your speech always be with grace, seasoned with salt, that you may know how you ought to answer each one.

2 Corinthians 4:15 (NIV) All this is for your benefit, so that the grace that is reaching more and more people may cause thanksgiving to overflow to the glory of God.

A believer must crave and align self to having a positive, plentiful supply of God's grace.

Luke 10:27 He answered, "Love the Lord your God with all your heart and with all your soul and with all your strength and with all your mind'[a]; and, 'Love your neighbor as yourself.'[b]"

For the believer in Christ, the mind certainly does matter a lot. It is expedient for the spiritual individual to look for the Divine, the higher purpose. The Spiritual individual should practice peace, empathy, connection, and reverence. These virtues release stress and tension and seek to serve in practical, valuable ways. We, believers, should experience the Divine daily through meditation in God's Word, reflection, relationship, fellowship, and communion.

Resist the ego- *2 Timothy 2:24-25* (NKJV) *"And the Lord's servant must not be quarrelsome but must be kind to everyone, able to teach, notresentful. Opponents must be gently instructed in the hope that God will grant them repentance leading them to a knowledge of the truth."*

Receive correction and instruction, accountability and support, teach, preach, rebuke, exhort, and correct; indeed, it is fitting for spiritual work to take place in the life and heart of a believer. Reflect on the Gospel daily. Christ's work and message are like anti-venom to the poison of selfish indifference and emotional ignorance.

Joshua 1:8(NKJV) Keep this Book of the Law always on your lips; meditate on it day and night, so that you may be careful to do everything written in it. Then you will be prosperous and successful.

A brief clue of Low Emotional Quotient (lack of sense or foolishness or folly), Emotional Quotient skill, and High

Emotional Quotient. It can be a barometer for measuring self.

Low EQ -Folly or foolishness- The fool deceives himself and pretends God doesn't see him or what he is doing. He acts as if there is no God.

Psalms 14:1 The fool[a] says in his heart, "There is no God." They are corrupt, their deeds are vile, there is no one who does good.

Proverbs 12:15 The way of fools seems right to them, but the wise listen to advice.

Proverbs 14:16 The wise fear the Lord and shun evil, but a fool is hotheaded and yet feels secure.

Proverbs 23:9 Do not speak to fools, for they will scorn your prudent words. (NIV)

Proverbs 28:26: Those who trust in themselves are fools, but those who walk in wisdom are kept safe.

EQ Skill- (self-awareness)- The ability to recognise and understand your moods, emotions, drives, and their effects on others.

High EQ (Wisdom)- The wise person lives life aware of themselves and God. He lives an honest life before God and in fear, health, and reverence of the Lord.

Proverbs 9:8-9 Do not rebuke mockers or they will hate you;

rebuke the wise and they will love you. Instruct the wise and they will be wiser still; teach the righteous and they will add to their learning.

Proverbs 15:31 Whoever heeds life-giving correction will be at home among the wise.

LOW EQ (FOLLY): The fool is emotionally out of control. He is quick to anger and shows little restraint in using his tongue to destroy himself and others.

Proverbs 10:8 The wise in heart accept commands, but a chattering fool comes to ruin.

Proverbs 12:23 The prudent keep their knowledge to themselves, but a fool's heart blurts out folly.

Proverbs 29:11 Fools give full vent to their rage but the wise bring calm in the end.

EQ Skill (SELF-REGULATION): The ability to control or redirect disruptive impulses and moods and the propensity to suspend judgement and think before acting.

HIGH EQ (WISDOM): The wise person is self-controlled. He does not give free vent to his anger or act emotionally out of control.

Proverbs 10:19 Sin is not ended by multiplying words, but the prudent hold their tongues.

Proverbs 16:21 The wise in heart are called discerning, and gracious words promote instruction.[a]

Low EQ (FOLY): The fool disregards the pain of others, even the pain caused by himself. He lives like a beast according to his animal instincts, without remorse and conscience.

Proverbs 14:20,21 & 31 The poor are shunned even by their neighbours, but the rich have many friends. It is a sin to despise one's neighbour, but blessed is the one who is kind to the needy. Whoever oppresses the poor shows contempt for their Maker, but whoever is kind to the needy honours God.

Proverbs 18:23: The poor plead for mercy, but the rich answer harshly.

EQ Skill (Social awareness): The ability to understand the emotional makeup of other people.

High EQ (WISDOM): the wise person care for the plight of others, realising the grace of God. He is compassionate and kind toward those less fortunate or privileged.

LOW EQ (FOLLY) The fool brings pain to his parents and those around him. He leaves a wake of relational devastation behind him.

Proverbs 13:20 Walk with the wise and become wise, for a companion of fools suffers harm.

Proverbs 17:21 & 25 To have a fool for a child brings grief;

there is no joy for the parent of a godless fool. A foolish son brings grief to his father and bitterness to the mother who bore him.

EQ Skill (Relational-management): A proficiency in managing relationships and building networks.

High EQ (wisdom) The person has the trust of others, even the King. He often prospers and rules over the foolish.

Proverbs 14:35 A king delights in a wise servant, but a shameful servant arouses his fury.

Proverbs 24:5 The wise prevail through great power, and those who have knowledge muster their strength.

Many of us rightly reject elevating feelings above truth but must be careful not to swing the pendulum to the other extreme. Managing and understanding the role of emotions is critical for every leader and believer, especially those shepherds and pastors and overseers, God's people. Unfortunately, numerous pastors would call emotional intelligence a feminine quality. Some even argue that men are the intellectual epicentre of the church and women are the emotional ones. This demeans emotional intelligence as unnecessary and, at worst, a liability reserved for women who can't control their tears.

CHAPTER 3

LIVING YOUR IDENTITY

Identity is one of the pivotal issues in natural and supernatural life; when you find it, you become dangerous to the onslaughts of the world around you. If people see contentment, joy, and genuine passion in you, they will be curious about what made you. But if all they see is a person with the same doom and gloom, they will not be interested in anything about you.

Everything you deal with in life, consciously or unconsciously, spiritual, or natural, visible, or invisible, questions your identity. In the natural, each time you meet new people, they want to know who you are, your name, where you come from, and what you do. Everything that confronts you in life will question your identity. The knowledge and ability of your identity give you resolve in life. Though in the natural, some people have double identities, they are in the daylight human and in the night devilish; in the day, doctors, and the night they are nurses or patients.

Just as your worship brings you into the presence of God, Satanic worship will bring you into the presence of Satan. Remember, worship is not just an activity in a church or synagogue; It is also the lifestyle you choose to live daily. Who are you really? Does your life and identity bring glory to God or Satan daily?

Acts 16:16-19 Now it happened, as we went to pray that a certain slave girl possessed with the spirit of divination met us, who brought her masters much profit by fortune-telling. This girl followed Paul and us and cried out, saying, "These men are the servants of the most High God, who proclaim to us the way of salvation. And this she did for many days. But Paul greatly annoyed, turned and said to the spirit, "I command you in the name of Jesus Christ to come out of her. And he came out that very hour. But when her masters saw that their hope of profit was gone, they seized Paul and Silas and dragged them into the marketplace to the authorities.

Even the devil recognizes your identity. Dogs recognise your identity. If a barking dog confronts you and you walk towards that dog, the dog recognises your dominion and quickly turns away. But if you become afraid of the barking dog and run, the dog will pursue you until he comes at you and bites. The dog recognizes when you are operating in dominion and losing your identity.

Acts 19:11-16 Now God worked unusual miracles by the hands of Paul so that even handkerchiefs or aprons were brought from his body to the sick and the diseases left them and evil spirits went out of them. Then some of the itinerant Jewish exorcists took it upon themselves to call the name of the Lord Jesus over those who had evil spirits, saying, "We exorcise you by the Jesus whom Paul preaches." Also there were sons of Sceva, a Jewish chief priest, who did so. And the evil spirit answered and said "Jesus I know and Paul I know but who are you? Then the man in whom the evil spirit was leaped on them, overpowered them and prevailed against them, so that they fled out of that house naked and wounded.

The way you are going is the way you choose consciously or unconsciously. Maybe you are in the wrong direction with your health issues, finances, feelings, emotions, spirituality, and how you do things daily as a Christian. What singles you out is how you live your identity. Emotions, health issues, financial crisis, depression, etc., are all asking questions, "WHO ARE YOU? Who you are and how you carry and react to these onslaughts gives you resolve or enslavement? Jesus, I know, Paul, I know but who are you? Who are you really?

CHAPTER 4

THE BOUNCE-BACK MENTALITY

Isaiah 54:17 (AMP) "No weapon that is formed against you will succeed; And every tongue that rises against you in judgment you will condemn. This [peace, righteousness, security, and triumph over opposition] is the heritage of the servants of the Lord, And this is their vindication from Me," says the Lord.

A well-developed sense of self-awareness (the ability to know yourself) makes you more effective in every other aspect of your life. By becoming more self-aware, you gain mastery and insight into why things happen to you the way they do and how you can increase your chances of creating circumstances favourable to success. Self-awareness is a skill to be developed. It makes much difference when you do; it puts you in a place of knowing yourself better.

Motivation should flow through like the phases of electrical current. Motivation should overpower you to overcome obstacles; push through challenges even when there is little external impetus to energize it. God wants you to have a failure-resistant brain and attitude; that is why you have His DNA and Nature. God supernaturally structured man in His likeness and Image that no adversity can incubate in Him. It would help if you did not let your fear or panic be more significant than your purpose. Don't be trapped in the paralysis of your analysis; your life goes in the direction your mind can transport. Our greatest enemy is not the devil but ignorance.

You should be able to perform well even when life is dull and unmotivated. Motivation is the fuel in the tank and the effort accelerator, the foot that presses down firmly on the gas pedal.

James 4:7 (AMP) So submit to [the authority of] God. Resist the devil [stand firm against him] and he will flee from you.

Winners understand and embrace the importance of failing, falling, and getting up faster than anyone else. The act of " getting -up," be it mentally or physically, equates to bouncing. Failing, falling, and getting up quickly is a bounce-back mentality. You often see this in boxers when knocked down and bleeding; they defy the oozing blood and pains of the wound to get up and get back to fight because they have the vision of winning while bleeding blood and pain. The motivated and resilient brain is about the big comeback from a big failure and not backing down and out or staying down when knocked down.

Philippians 4:13 (AMP) I can do all things [which He has called me to do] through Him who strengthens and empowers me [to fulfill His purpose—I am self-sufficient in Christ's sufficiency; I am ready for anything and equal to anything through Him who infuses me with inner strength and confident peace.]

Possess a highly evolved sense of self-awareness. When you narrow the gap between your public and authentic self, it is easier to read how others experience you. You can use yourself as a stimulator to understand others. Winners with a real sense of self recognise healthy boundaries and know when to be an open book and when to close it up and put it on the shelf. Don't be the radio that advertises your adversity.

Be brutally honest with yourself, identify your weakness, and learn to minimise it; this way, you avoid the sand traps. Self-awareness is critical for maintaining a prosperous calibrated talent meter. You have the potential to become a great public speaker, a fantastic parent, an author, or an incredible teacher. Still, if you don't recognise the abilities within yourself, you won't take the time to develop your natural talents. All the hard work in the world won't turn you into a master director if that sort of endeavour doesn't play to your strength.

Everyone will face obstacles, but if you want to experience

prosperity, you must keep moving ahead, doing something and doing it with passion. Winning in life has little to do with how smart you are, your high intelligence, your circumstances, your financial resources, or your luck. It all zeroes to your tenacity to create a failure-resistant attitude in every circumstance. Anytime you discover who God has made you be, you become a threat to the giants in your life. To function in God`s Image, the giants in your life have to die; when you realize God's power, you will search for the giants in your life to kill.

Romans 8:37-39 (NIV) No, in all these things we are more than conquerors through him who loved us. For I am convinced that neither death nor life, neither angels nor demons,[a] neither the present nor the future, nor any powers, neither height nor depth, nor anything else in all creation, will be able to separate us from the love of God that is in Christ Jesus our Lord.

The Word of God is the only living thing that will calibrate your level of focus for the task at your hand. The Word of God is your effort-accelerator. People with exceptional opportunity radar recognize that opportunities don't always come gift-wrapped; more often than not, they come wrapped in a problem or an idea everyone else has simply missed. Sometimes they come wrapped in your weakness; sometimes, your destiny is wrapped up in the situation you go through; when you confront it, you unveil your destiny. It would be best if you craved the tenacity to confront what confronts you.

You don't incubate circumstances; you confront them. You learn to avoid mistakes by slowing down and taking the time to assess the pros and cons of each opportunity. When you stumble, your skin grows thicker with the confidence to carry on to a higher level. There are distractions that compete for attention constantly. A winner's brain can focus on tasks and activities that are vital in the moment, especially when the moment is full of environmental stressors and distractions. You can deliberately calibrate your focus level under a wide variety of circumstances. If you don't realize you have gaps in your abilities, it will never occur to you to try and make improvements; even great talents have opportunities for improvement.

A man may become the master of his destiny because he has the power to influence his subconscious mind. One person's indulgence is another person's essential component of a good life, and neither is right nor wrong. The diversity simply reflects the impact of individual perspectives on the meaning of prosperity.

Poverty is a state of mind and the absence of a financial condition. You can have money and still be poor. Poverty, therefore, is not just the absence of money. , mmm. Your perceptions and beliefs matter. Success is achievable if you choose it and work at it. But if you don't choose it or believe it, you most likely will not have success. You must work on yourself, your attitude, your beliefs, and your thinking or thought pattern. If you believe it is possible, then do it.

Your current thoughts are creating your future life. What you think about or focus on the most will appear in your life. Whatever method one uses, a new state of mind must be put into practice through faith or cognitive behavioral pattern to move forward in life and achieve something more significant. Trust yourself, and create the kind of self you will be happy to live with all your life. Make the most of yourself by fanning the tiny inner sparks of your personality into flames of achievement. Everyone should look for a single spark of individuality that makes them different from others and develop it. Don't let your spark be lost; it is your only real claim of importance.

Turning setbacks and adversity into lessons is one of the most powerful ways to speed progress toward a goal, gain the strength to carry on, and create a better life. Because of an exaggerated fear of making mistakes, people who lack self-esteem avoid taking risks. These unfortunate tendencies sabotage success, acting like internally constructed obstacles to achieving a fulfilling and prosperous life.

It is not possible to grant another person an authentic and durable sense of self-esteem. It is a quality that we gain through our own experiences. We can create a life where we can prosper by staying conscious of who we are and what we want; this requires an internal compass to navigate us based on our genuine selves and our broader goals. To find an inner compass, we must reflect on and acknowledge the personal values that we hold dearly.

Prosperity can and must encompass the unique values and goals that define your dreams. Failures and stumbles may be among our best teachers on the pathway to self-esteem. According to research studies, human beings have an innate resiliency that can turn challenges into opportunities for growth.

Acts 16:26 (NIV) Suddenly there was such a violent earthquake that the foundations of the prison were shaken. At once all the prison doors flew open, and everyone's chains came loose.

Acts 2:2 (NIV) Suddenly a sound like the blowing of a violent wind came from heaven and filled the whole house where they were sitting.

Suddenly doors are opening on your behalf as your foundations are shaken. Suddenly breakthroughs are yours as the blowing of the violent wind fills your house and strengthens you to become a witness of God's manifestations.

We must be willing to let go of the old judgments, opinions, and worn-out attitudes that limit us. A change requires taking stock and recognizing our creative responsibility. If we stay stocked in the old concepts and do not take action, we may seek vicarious fulfilment or comforts but will never have the sweet taste of success.

An effective way to build self-esteem is by raising our awareness of how we think and make a conscious habit of replacing negative language with positive ones when thinking and speaking about ourselves and others. Surrounding oneself with positive messages and successful and happy people are powerful methods for increasing one's sense of self-worth.

Wealth is defined as an abundance of valuable material possessions or resources. Wealth cannot be defined strictly in terms of finances. Some people are wealthy in family, rich in health, wealthy in love, or wealthy in friendship. You could have money and not have good health, friends, family, love, etc. Wealth is having what you want in life.

An unexamined life is not worth living. By making an effort to consider where we stand in life and where we want to go, we begin to evolve and move forward to a higher altitude. If we do not examine the conscious and subconscious beliefs that drive us, life can become an endless pattern of unconscious repetition. We can also predict that the items we consider luxuries today will be considered ordinary conveniences tomorrow.

CHAPTER 5

THE TRICHOTOMY OF HUMAN BEINGS

Just as there is a revealed doctrine of God in the Bible, there is also a revealed doctrine of man. The locus classicus; man, is a spirit; he has a soul and lives in a body. These three dimensions of man's being are not three distinct and independent entities or parts of man. They are three processes of looking at the unity in man, the unity in three different aspects: flesh, soul, and spirit. The distinction between soul and spirit is crucial in spiritual discernment.

Man is a tripartite being. Many believers who love the Lord Jesus and seek to grow in Him are ignorant of the nature of their being: that they were created tripartite: spirit, soul, and body. There is a big misconception that the spirit and soul are synonymous, but the Bible reveals that man is tripartite, explicitly in 1 Thessalonians 5:23 "Now may the God of peace Himself sanctify you completely: and may your whole spirit, (pneüma), soul (psyche) and body (söma) be preserved blameless at the coming of our Lord Jesus Christ."

Genesis 2:7," And the Lord God formed man of the dust of the ground and breathed into his nostrils the breath of life; and man became a living soul."

The Lord formed man from the dust (body), breathed the breath of life (spirit) and man became a living soul. The soul is what connects the spiritual realm with the physical as the body gives us worldly consciousness, the soul self-consciousness, and the spirit God-consciousness.

Psalms 139:14 I will praise you; for I am fearfully and wonderfully made; marvelous are your works; and that my soul knows right well.

THE SOUL: The soul is the spiritual part of a person which continues existing after the body is dead. The term soul stands for the totality of self and person, your individuality, yourself, and the psychology in you. The soul is self-conscious, tantamount to speaking about oneself or ego. It is man's interior (infra). The soul is the body form that makes a man uniquely what he is. It comprises intellect, will, and emotions. It is the very principle of life; it is the seat of man's personality in which sense comprises not only his consciousness but also sub-consciousness and unconscious life (In the psychological sense). Hence the soul is the abode of emotions; man's rationality and ability to make decisions do not cancel out his sensitivity. When you hurt me, I react; it is your soul that gets emotional. It is your soul that worries about a situation. You can master every situation in your soul and memories, the good, the bad, and the ugly. You can think yourself up, or you can think yourself down all in your soul. Your soul is the part that says "I am" made in God's image, your heart. It cannot be killed by any man. *Matthew 10:28 And fear not them which can kill the body but are not able to kill the soul but rather fear Him which is able to destroy both the soul and the body in hell.* Your soul leaves your body when you are physically dead.

Genesis 35:18 And it came to pass, as her soul was departing, (for she died) that she called his name Ben-oni: but his father called him Benjamin.

Your soul differs from the spirit and body. The soul consists of three parts: mind, will, and emotion; with the mind, one knows and remembers. Lamentation 3:20a "My soul still remembers" and Psalm 139:14b "And that my soul knows very well."

The will is the part of the soul that houses the choosing and refusing functions, choices, and indecisions. *Job 7:15 "So that my soul chooses strangling and death rather than my body" Job 6:7 "My soul refuses to touch them: they are as loathsome food to me."*

And finally, emotions are part of the soul that expresses human feelings such as joy, peace, and sorrow.

Psalm 23:3 "He restores my soul; expresses joy Psalm" 19:7 "The law of the Lord is perfect, converting the soul." Matthew 26:38, "My soul is exceedingly sorrowful, even to death," expresses sorrow, *and Job 7:11, "Therefore I will not restrain my mouth; I will speak in the anguish of my spirit; I will complain in the bitterness of my soul."*

The soul has spiritual desires and craves, like thirsting for God. Psalm 42:1-2 *As the deer pants for the waters brooks, so pants my soul for you, O God vs2 My soul thirsts for God, for the living God. When shall I come and appear before God?*

The soul seeks God Deuteronomy 6:5 *"You shall love the Lord your God with all your heart, with all your soul and with all your strength. Deuteronomy 4:29 "But from there you will seek the Lord your God, and you will find Him if you seek Him with all your heart and with all your soul.*

With our soul, you fear and serve God. Deuteronomy 10:12, *"And now, Israel, what does the Lord your God require of you, but to fear the Lord your God, to walk in all His ways and to love Him, to serve the Lord your God with all your heart and with all your soul."*

What God does for the soul; *Psalm 49:15 But God will redeem my soul from the power of the grave, for He shall receive me.*

God delivers your soul; Psalm 56:13 For You have delivered my soul from death, Have You not kept my feet from falling, That I may walk before God in the light of the living. And finally, god saves the soul of man; 1 Peter 1:9 receiving the end of your faith- the salvation of your souls.

THE SPIRIT: The spirit is that part of the human being that is not physical but relates to the most profound thoughts and feelings. The spirit man is considered conscious of God and open to Him. This is called the "Superior Portion" of the soul here; you enter into the domain of the "Supernatural". The spirit is the core, the most profound dimension of man's being, which Apostle Paul describes as "the inner or interior man

(2 Corinthians 4:16, Ephesians 3:16). The interior man is where the regenerating Spirit moves him, where Christ dwells through faith, and where that love that comes from Christ is born. It is by Man's spiritual dimension, of his having a human spirit (the breath of God in him), that he is a living soul. The spirit is the ultimate principle of man's life. When it is breathed into the body, life begins.

It is a question of that secret and intimate part of man, the part that is spirit open to God. The spirit of man is the immaterial part of a human being. It is the part that gives man the ability to relate with God. The human spirit consists of three parts: conscience, fellowship, and intuition. The conscience is the part that either condemns or justifies. It enables human beings to perceive right or wrong. Romans 8:16 The spirit Himself bears witness with our spirit that we are children of God. Through fellowship, you can relate with God; John 4:24 "God is Spirit, and those who worship Him, must worship in spirit and truth. And by intuition, man can feel something even though he may have no proof or evidence. Here emanates faith. God can give direct or precise knowledge which is virtually independent of reason or situation. 1 Corinthians 2:11 For what man knows the things of a man except the spirit of the man which is in him? Even so no one knows the things of God except the spirit of God.

The spirit is the God-consciousness in you. It is the part that relates to either God or the devil. The spirit of man can be good or evil, light or darkness, holy or unholy, clean, or unclean, of God or Satan. *Luke 9:55 But He turned and rebuked them, and said, "You do not know what manner of spirit you are of."*

THE BODY: The body is man's considered material that relates to the rest of the physical universe. Apostle Paul calls it "the outer man" (1 Corinthians 4:16). Through the body, man gathers information and deals with the world around him. There is nothing evil about the body itself; what is evil, however, is man's attempt to satisfy himself by living primarily or exclusively for the pleasures of the body (Romans 1:24-25).

The body of a human being has five senses with which man

contacts the physical world. The sight, smell, hearing, taste, and feeling. These enable humans to exist in this physical and material world.

The soul helps humans to relate with the body as it also helps them to connect with the spirit. In other words, the soul is the spokesman and the middleman between the spirit and the body. By yielding the soul to God, the body can be subdued and automatically responds to the things of the spirit. But when the soul is not spiritually alive, it will be impossible to win the body to respond positively to the spirit. Its spiritual nature at any time, whether spiritually alive or dead, determines the nature of the body and spirit. This is because the power of the will to choose is there, and the body, the spirit, and God respect that. This is where the power of freelance is displayed and expressed.

Your body houses your soul and spirit. Your body is the container and clothing for the soul and spirit. It can be killed because it is earthly and remains here on earth after one is dead. You cannot build up your spirit and neglect your body because it is your body that makes you available in the world. It is your body that gives you a royal consciousness in the world. If you lose your body, you lose your royal consciousness.

"I am wonderfully made." The first is over your mind. What happens in your head is the battle of the mind. You don't have to be old to be tired. When you are tired, your engine is exhausted because of the usage. When you worry too much, your engine will be tired. It is not the years that make you tired; it is not your age that makes you constantly tired; it is the mileage. You get tired because of how you use your mind and thoughts. You get tired because your soul is tired. Yourself is tired of everything. It is not the year in which a car is made that makes the car an old one, but how many miles the vehicle has travelled makes it an old one. Nobody wants to buy an old car. If you live with threats in life, you cannot achieve anything. If you get threats to walk with you, you cannot get out.

You cannot make a great decision when you are tired of life. You walk only in your reality. You begin to think of things that are, in reality, not there. Your perception is off; you begin to write the book only you can read. When your emotions are exhausted, you walk into the reality of your thinking. When you say it is love, it is love; they don't love when you say it is not love. Many times, you think people don't love you because they are not speaking your language, the language that you are accustomed to, because you always get to define what love is based on your weary perceptions, which is a result of your dysfunction and that is why nobody can love you enough because until you define love on the personal dysfunction, you have nothing that makes meaning to you.

When you get a hole in your soul, nobody can love you enough to fill it. This is why you need to stop and be healed of your malfunction. You cannot trust yourself, you cannot trust your perception, you cannot trust your judgment, and you cannot trust your attitude, all because there is a dysfunction in you; you will always find fault in other people and think you are the reason why they exist because there is a hole in your soul. You cannot be a child of God and at the same time dysfunction in your soul; you cannot be a child of God and have a wound in your soul.

Some people say words that change a situation, while others speak words that change destiny. Those who change destiny are nation shakers. The pinnacle of your truth is that which leads you to a place of sovereignty, where any situation or circumstances cannot move you. You have a fixed position in this stead because of the authority of the word. If you conceive the invisible, you can do the impossible. God uses a submitted life to accomplish the impossible.

1 John 3:1-2 Behold, what manner of love the Father has bestowed upon us, that we should be called sons of God: therefore the world knows us not, because it knew Him not vs2 beloved now we are the sons of God and it does not yet appear what we shall be: but we know that when he shall appear, we shall be like Him; for we shall see Him as he is.

You cannot be a pastor, a prophet, evangelist, teacher, etc., and have a wound in your soul. You must get up by yourself; God will compensate you for what life didn't give you. God will balance your books and say, I will bless you anyway.

Stop letting people who do little for you and in your life control so much of your mind, feelings, and emotions. Confront your past and think positively.

Genesis 9:2 -3 And the fear of you and the dread of you shall be upon every beast of the earth and upon every fowl of the air, upon all that moves upon the earth and upon all the fishes of the sea; into your hand are they delivered. Every moving thing that lives shall be meat for you; even as the green herb, have I given you all things.

CHAPTER 6

PERSONIFIED IDENTITY

God is perfection personified because He is the standard for measuring rightness.

The only reason things keep you in a crisis mode, troubles, hardships, ugly attitude, sickness, depression, and life struggles is ignorance of your identity. The problem with today's world is that everybody has become an expert on somebody's life except their own. The emptiness of an open heart creates a cavity for God to fill, but a closed mind never receives anything from God. The only difference between you and the person you envy or admire is their perspective on life and themselves.

It is who you are, your definition of self, that super-drives you to the right perspective, and a right view locates your destiny. Don't allow people and anything to anchor you down and leave you limited so that they can have fellowship and you can have failure. You are created to be solution oriented. This is a sovereign declaration of a sovereign God that you be solution oriented. What it means, in other words, is that it has been passed into divine law, so you must discover your supernatural identity to enable you to regain absolute control of your destiny.

Genesis 9:2 (NKJV) And the fear of you and the dread of you shall be on every beast of the earth, on every bird of the air, on all that move on the earth, and on all the fish of the sea. They are given into your hand.

If you are disciplined in your perspective, you will come out victoriously. It is arrogance for a finite mind, an ordinary natural mind, to think that he understands an infinite God. We need to go before God daily to get new information and insights and have more clarity because sometimes we walk away hearing what God said, but we do not understand what He meant.

There are always accusers and mockers in your life because accusing is what the devil does best to steal your identity.

Revelation 12:10 (NKJV) Then I heard a loud voice saying in heaven, "Now salvation, and strength, and the kingdom of our God, and the power of His Christ have come, for the accuser of our brethren, who accused them before our God day and night, has been cast down.

You cannot regain control of your destiny if you assign your blame game to people. If you ended up where you are right now because of people, you have no power to fix it yourself; they must fix it. Refrain from your blame game so that you can fix things when they go wrong. Don't forget that God gets glory from every hardship and storm in your life; God can be glorified in something that does not seem beautiful because your vision is not His.

Acts 19:11-17 (NKJV) Now God worked unusual miracles by the hands of Paul, so that even handkerchiefs or aprons were brought from his body to the sick, and the diseases left them and the evil spirits went out of them. Then some of the itinerant Jewish exorcists took it upon themselves to call the name of the Lord Jesus over those who had evil spirits, saying, [a] "We [b]exorcise you by the Jesus whom Paul preaches." Also there were seven sons of Sceva, a Jewish chief priest, who did so. And the evil spirit answered and said, "Jesus I know, and Paul I know; but who are you?" Then the man in whom the evil spirit was leaped on them, [c]overpowered them, and prevailed against [d]them, so that they fled out of that house naked and wounded. This became known both to all Jews and Greeks dwelling in Ephesus; and fear fell on them all, and the name of the Lord Jesus was magnified.

When you understand what God created you for and His sovereignty, you cease to operate at the base level of an ordinary man. The moment you perceive God's definition of yourself, you become invincible and begin seeing and understanding everything with the eyes of the Spirit. When you are filled with the Spirit of God, you will be enabled supernaturally to do every impossibility.

Ephesians 1:17-18 (NKJV) that the God of our Lord Jesus Christ, the Father of glory, may give to you the spirit of wisdom and revelation in the knowledge of Him, the eyes of your [a]understanding being enlightened; that you may know what is the hope of His calling, what are the riches of the glory of His inheritance in the saints,

God has recreated a believer with a purpose to possess and rule over every impossibility because the believer is linked with God by divine birth; the believer is His likeness and His image. This divine mystery is about a believer the devil is after, and he accuses you to make you forget who you are and what you are created for.

Ephesians 5:18 (NKJV)And do not be drunk with wine, in which is dissipation; but be filled with the Spirit,

When you are drunk with wine, you are not in control; you stagger, and the wine and the level of alcohol in your system control everything about you from your mindset, movement, and vocabulary. You lose your selfhood because there are influences that want to dismantle who you are and the purpose of God for your life.

1 Corinthians 2:9-15 (NKJV) But as it is written: "Eye has not seen, nor ear heard, Nor have entered into the heart of man The things which God has prepared for those who love Him." But God has revealed them to us through His Spirit. For the Spirit searches all things, yes, the deep things of God. For what man knows the things of a man except for the spirit of the man in him? Even so no one knows the things of God except the Spirit of God. Now we have received, not the spirit of the world, but the Spirit who is from God, that we might know the things that have been freely given to us by God. These things we also speak, not in words which man's wisdom teaches but which the [a]Holy Spirit teaches, comparing spiritual things with spiritual. But the natural man does not receive the things of the Spirit of God, for they are foolishness to him; nor can he know them, because they are spiritually discerned. But he who is spiritual, judges all things, yet he himself is rightly judged by no one.

The problem of a believer is ignorance of who God made him be and what God created Him for. You may have problems but thank God problems do not have you. Every hard time you go through has come to manifest God's glory and showcases really who you are. Every trial, storm, flood, and fire you pass through in life will reveal your identity. Who you perceive yourself to be determines where you end up with what you are confronted with.

Isaiah 43:10 (NKJV) "You are My witnesses," says the Lord, "And My servant whom I have chosen, That you may know and believe Me, And understand that I am He. Before Me there was no God formed, Nor shall there be after Me.

It does not matter what name, tag, and definition people put on you, remember you are still a person of purpose and destiny if you have Christ. You are not a passerby; you are the likeness and image of God; you are a son and a daughter adopted by Most High God. Each time you stand before people, what reflects is the glory of God because you are God's glory.

John 17:22-23 (NIV) I have given them the glory that you gave me, that they may be one as we are one— I in them and you in me—so that they may be brought to complete unity. Then the world will know that you sent me and have loved them even as you have loved me.

The glory is not for decoration; the glory was given to you to be God's representative in the everyday scene, especially today's scene. When you declare your identity before men, the power of God is released through you into that atmosphere and enhances your spiritual growth. It is an honour and a joyful thing to be identified with Christ.

Luke 9:26-27 (NIV) Whoever is ashamed of me and my words, the Son of Man will be ashamed of them when he comes in his glory and the glory of the Father and the holy angels. "Truly I tell you, some who are standing here will not taste death before they see the kingdom of God."

The revelation of your divine identity will transform you into an instrument through which the Name of God is magnified. God wants to uproot the self-centred you to get Himself into you.

2 Corinthians 2:14-15 (NKJV) Now thanks be to God who always leads us in triumph in Christ, and through us diffuses the fragrance of His knowledge in every place. For we are to God, the fragrance of Christ among those who are being saved and among those who are perishing.

The God in you must come out, reflect, and reign over circumstances and every dominion. Who are you? Is the question separating you from your natural and supernatural, sickness and good health, poverty, richness, etc.? Are you just who you are because of what people call you or think of you?

Genesis 2:7 (NKJV) And the Lord God formed man of the dust of the ground, and breathed into his nostrils the breath of life; and man became a living being.

19 Out of the ground the Lord God formed every beast of the field and every bird of the air, and brought *them* to [a]Adam to see what he would call them. And whatever Adam called each living creature, that *was* its name.

Every problem in your life is a living creature; sickness is a living creature, poverty is a living creature, depression, cancer, etc.; whatever you name them is whatever they become. You have been given the potential to call, reprove, rebuke, repeal, uproot and destroy every opposition to your life; whatever name you call, what confronts you is what they become.

Ecclesiastes 7:7 (NKJV) Surely oppression destroys a wise man's reason, And a bribe [a]debases the heart 12 For wisdom is a defense as money is a defense, But the [excellence of knowledge is that wisdom gives life to those who have it.

God's intent for humanity is that people become what His dictates are, live it, and manifest it. You cannot become the dictates of God when you are ignorant of whom He says you are.

Isaiah 13:12 (KJV) I will make a man more precious than fine gold; even a man than the golden wedge of Ophir.

Psalm 82:6 (NKJV) I said, "You are [a]gods, And all of you are children of the Most High.

John 10:34 (NKJV) Jesus answered them, "Is it not written in your law, 'I said, "You are gods"'?

The emphasis on "you are gods" amplifies the fact that God gave humanity dominion and reign on the earth over every circumstance because man was created in His likeness, and man has the DNA of God.

What will your intent and consciousness be after hearing this message and discovering that God wants you to reign and has given you the potential and power to manifest His authority in your atmosphere? Are you going to define yourself through the dictates of God? Will you be defined and described by circumstances and people around you?

Psalm 139:14 (NKJV) I will praise You, for [a]I am fearfully and wonderfully made; Marvelous are Your works, And that my soul knows very well.

CHAPTER 7

SELF-ESTEEM BECOMES YOUR VALUE

A Christian has untapped realms of ability, giftedness, and potential, waiting for one touch, one moment, one collision of God's power. Your journey began before birth, and it is time to embrace it. God is calling your life to experience a shift, a change, a transition, and a promotion. When your potential is realized and released, your purpose for life will manifest. We must start mining the multi-dimensional observable principles in our lives.

Genesis 1:26 (NIV) Then God said, "Let us make mankind in our image, in our likeness, so that they may rule over the fish in the sea and the birds in the sky, over the livestock and all the wild animals, [and over all the creatures that move along the ground."

1 Peter 2:9 (NIV) But you are a chosen people, a royal

priesthood, a holy nation, God's special possession, that you may declare the praises of him who called you out of darkness into his wonderful light.

A Christian has untapped realms of ability, giftedness, and potential, waiting for one touch, one moment, one collision of God's power. Your journey began before birth, and it is time to embrace it. God is calling your life to experience a shift, a change, a transition, and a promotion. When your potential is realized and released, your purpose for life will manifest. We must start mining the multi-dimensional observable principles in our lives.

Jeremiah 1:5 (NIV) "Before I formed you in the womb I knew you before you were born I set you apart; I appointed you as a prophet to the nations."

The value of your creator, whose Image you are, should cause you to reconsider your worth and value. You are handcrafted in the Image of God; you were custom-made, void of purposelessness. You were allowed access into this dimension of life by the nod of the Creator God that you would be strategically placed at this time, at this age, in your gender, in your ethnicity with your gifting, and with your talent for God's divine purpose.

Ephesians 1:4-6 (NIV) For he chose us in him before the creation of the world to be holy and blameless in his sight. In love he predestined us for adoption to sonship through

Jesus Christ, in accordance with his pleasure and will— to the praise of his glorious grace, which he has freely given us in the One he loves.

Self–Esteem is a fundamental human need. Self-Esteem and Self–Respect seem to be prerequisites for achieving a life of true wealth and prosperity. When we have a solid sense of Self-Esteem, we feel strong and confident in our ability to cope with life's challenges, and we can function at a high level with a sense of control over life. We can expect a measure of success because we know we can be effective.

Jeremiah 1:5 (NIV) "Before I formed you in the womb I knew you before you were born I set you apart; I appointed you as a prophet to the nations."

Self-esteem is a vital combination of two qualities- Self-confidence and Self-respect. Self–respect may be an essential component of self-esteem. With Self-respect, we see ourselves as worthy and deserving of happiness, achievement, and love. Self-esteem is the immune system of consciousness or conscious mind.

Those with solid self-esteem are resilient in the face of life's difficulties. People who are comfortable with themselves and their achievements take pleasure in being who they are. They face each new challenge with a few deep breaths and a measure of confidence that they will succeed despite all odds. As they achieve each new goal, their self-respect grows and their ability to fulfill their potential with it.

John 15:15-16 (NIV) I no longer call you servants, because a servant does not know his master's business. Instead, I have called you friends, for everything I learned from my Father I have made known to you. You did not choose me, but I chose you and appointed you so that you might go and bear fruit—fruit that will last—and so that whatever you ask in my name the Father will give you.

When our basic human needs for self-esteem and self-respect are not met, we give up easily, blame others, strive for less, and often fail to achieve our goals. Arrogance, self-righteousness, manipulation, and boastfulness portray low self-esteem, primarily in extroverts; such behaviours are futile attempts to compensate for a sense of unworthiness. Other signs of low self-esteem are a tendency to criticize oneself heavily and dissatisfaction with one's performance.

For introverts' poor self-esteem may be manifested as an excessive desire to please others and reluctance to say no out of fear of causing displeasure. People who lack self-esteem avoid taking risks because of an exaggerated fear of making mistakes. These unfortunate tendencies sabotage success, acting like internally constructed obstacles to achieving a fulfilling and prosperous life.

Psalm 139:14 (NIV) I praise you because I am fearfully and wonderfully made; your works are wonderful, I know that full well.

It is impossible to grant another person an authentic and durable sense of self-esteem. It is a quality that we gain through our own experiences. You are not a cosmic accident; you were handcrafted and custom-made by God. The value of your creator should cause you to revalue your worth and value. Once you realize that you were created on purpose and in the Image of God, you begin to recognize that secrets are stored inside you. God the Creator is multi-dimensional enough to make you uniquely. Trust this design; the moment you start to embrace how you have been formed and fashioned is when you step into the purpose you were created for.

God is not the author of prolonged purposelessness. You might be. One of the most prevalent enemies to your stepping into your purpose is the downright deception that "the grass is greener." Everything about you was designed with intentionality. Your design is directed and connected to your purpose. If you neglect your design and refuse to celebrate how you were made, you will never step into who you were made to be.

Isaiah 43:1&4 (NIV) But now, this is what the Lord says— he who created you, Jacob, he who formed you, Israel: "Do not fear, for I have redeemed you; I have summoned you by name; you are mine. Since you are precious and honored in my sight, and because I love you, I will give people in exchange for you, nations in exchange for your life.

Whatever you think you can do or believe you can do, begin to do it. Actions have magic, grace, and power in them. Creating our own stories starts with action; with small steps and seemingly small choice we make each day. Once we begin, each step can be golden. Your environment colours your mindset. This operating system specifically affects your attitudes, beliefs, faith, success, wealth, language, and tenacity to do and be. The programming you receive can significantly condition you for better or worse.

Romans 12:2 (NIV) Do not conform to the pattern of this world, but be transformed by the renewing of your mind. Then you will be able to test and approve what God's will is—his good, pleasing and perfect will.

A man may become the master of his destiny because he has the power to influence his subconscious mind. To be poor is a state of mind and a financial condition. Your perceptions and beliefs matter. Success is achievable if you choose it and work for it. Your current thoughts are creating your future. Although it is the rare individual who scales the summit of true greatness in any field, taking the steps toward our own goals calls upon what is most remarkable in us.

How should we build self–esteem? By raising awareness of how we think and making a conscious habit of replacing negative language with positive language when thinking and speaking about ourselves and others.

Proverbs 6:2 (NIV) you have been trapped by what you said, ensnared by the words of your mouth.

Surround yourself with positive-minded people, messages, and successful and happy people, increasing your sense of worth. Simply by being alive, we are worthy. It can be strengthened if our sense of self is damaged, battered, or fragile. Self-esteem is something that we can learn and build upon. And one of the best ways to learn is by doing it. The way to create self–esteem in us is through accomplishments. When we accomplish something somewhat difficult, creative, or challenging, we demonstrate to our harshest critics that we are capable. These accomplishments can be small, yet if we realize them, even if we occasionally fall on our faces, we experience our capacity to achieve and develop inner strength and tenacity.

Going through this step-by-step process is the most powerful thing we can do to build our self-esteem and self-respect. Failures and stumbles may be among our best teachers on the path to self-esteem. Many studies highlight the potentially strengthening effects of adversity. Humans can turn challenges and setbacks into opportunities for growth. Turning setbacks and adversity into lessons is one of the most powerful ways to speed up progress toward a goal to gain the strength to carry on and create a better life.

Trust yourself. Create the kind of self you will be and make the most of yourself by fanning the tiny inner spark of possibility into flames of achievements. Another critical factor in establishing self-esteem and self-worth is finding an avenue for expressing something you love. Love is expansive, attractive, and cohesive. If you love what you do, you are going to work harder, you are going to try harder, you are going to be better at it, and you are going to enjoy your life doing it more. Everything in your life exists because you first chose something. Choices are at the root of every one of your results. Each option starts a behaviour that, over time, becomes a habit.

Success will not come to you if you do not fight for it. You can't try something and say it doesn't work just because it has not worked yet; it's about never quitting. You should never quit. Choices add up to habits that produce either a prosperous life or a life that is something less than we want it to be. Essentially, you make your choices, and then your choices make you. No matter how slight, every decision alters the trajectory of your life. Ultimately, our lives reflect the conscious and unconscious choices we make each day.

The river's strength is gained through momentum by the focus of the flow in one direction. We can use that momentum to move toward our dreams and our goals. Accepting responsibility allows us to persist, despite obstacles and setbacks. We become the stream that moves forward despite all the twists, turns, and rocks in our way. No matter our situation or challenge, we can decide how to respond. We can feel victimized and resigned and give others power over our lives, or we can take personal responsibility for our choices.

To live a more prosperous life, we must accept responsibility. You must crave personal responsibility. You cannot change circumstances, the seasons, or the wind, but you can change yourself. That is something you must long to change. The qualities that make life prosperous are intensely personal and subjective, the experiences that bring meaning, focus, and results.

CHAPTER 8

COGNITIVE-BEHAVIOUR/ FAITH

God wants us as Christians to have and search for the transcendent level of knowledge that is above and beyond the range of normal or physical human experience. A partaker of a divine nature must operate and function in a supernatural atmosphere.

Ephesians 1:17-18 (NKJV) that the God of our Lord Jesus Christ, the Father of glory, may give to you the spirit of wisdom and revelation in the knowledge of Him, the eyes of your [a]understanding being enlightened; that you may know what is the hope of His calling, what are the riches of the glory of His inheritance in the saints,

Cognitive-behaviour therapy states that human difficulties emanate or stem from thought. It is not the event but a person's belief that causes emotional stress or disturbance. This therapy aims to challenge irrational thoughts and help individuals separate their self-evaluation from their evaluation of their behaviour. In other words, the central goal is to differentiate one's identity from one's actions. Rather than being what you do, you are a being who does things. Cognitive-behaviour therapy encourages individuals to accept themselves despite their flaws, imperfections, or shortcomings.

Hebrews 11:1 & 6 (NKJV) Now faith is the [a]substance of things hoped for, the [b]evidence of things not seen. But without faith it is impossible to please Him, for he who comes to God must believe that He is and that He is a rewarder of those who diligently seek Him.

Faith comes from the Greek word "PISTIS" and believe from the verb "PISTUEO."

Faith means belief, firm persuasion, assurance, firm conviction, and faithfulness; belief -Pistueo - means to trust in and rely on, commit to the charge of, confide in and have a mental persuasion. Faith is a supernatural currency that makes things available in the spiritual realm before manifesting in the physical. Faith does not exist on the premises of the five senses and is not natural. It is not natural for you to have faith, but faith is what comes into you through the supernatural Word of God and gives you control of your environment. Faith makes you function extraordinarily. Faith is the soil on which God's Word is planted.

Romans 10:17 (NKJV) So then faith comes by hearing, and hearing by the word of God.

Hebrews 11:32-37 (NKJV) And what more shall I say? For the time would fail me to tell of Gideon and Barak and Samson and Jephthah, also *of* David and Samuel and the prophets: who through faith subdued kingdoms, worked righteousness, obtained promises, stopped the mouths of lions, quenched the violence of fire, escaped the edge of the sword, out of weakness were made strong, became valiant in battle, turned to fight the armies of the aliens. Women received their dead raised to life again. Others were tortured, not accepting deliverance that they might obtain a better resurrection. Still, others had trials of mocking, scourging, chains, and imprisonment. They were stoned, sawn in two, [a]were tempted, and slain with the sword. They wandered about in sheepskins and goatskins, being destitute, afflicted, tormented—

Romans 4:19-21 (KJV) And being not weak in faith, he considered not his own body now dead, when he was about an hundred years old, neither yet the deadness of Sarah's womb: He staggered not at the promise of God through unbelief; but was strong in faith, giving glory to God; And being fully persuaded that, what he had promised, he was able also to perform.

Cognitive-behaviour therapy is based on the perspective that humans have the potential for rational and irrational thought.

People are prone to positives such as happiness, love, thought, self-preservation, growth, and self-actualisation; they are also prone to negative like repeated mistakes, intolerance, avoidance of thought, self-blame, and self-destruction. Cognitive-behaviour therapists use an ABC-DEF model comprising an activating event that leads to a belief that leads to emotional and behavioural consequences. The circle is broken by a disputing intervention, leading to an effect and a new feeling. In essence, a human emotional disturbance is thought to result from internalising negative thoughts. Cognitive restructuring makes self-improvement possible as irrational thoughts are replaced with constructive thinking.

Romans 12:2 (NKJV) And do not be conformed to this world, but be transformed by the renewing of your mind, that you may prove what is that good and acceptable and perfect will of God.

2 Corinthians 10:5 (NKJV) casting down arguments and every high thing that exalts itself against the knowledge of God, bringing every thought into captivity to the obedience of Christ,

If our minds as Christians are not firmly grounded in the truth, which is God's Word, then we are more susceptible or vulnerable to deceptions.

James 2:14 (NKJV) What does it profit, my brethren, if someone says he has faith but does not have works? Can faith save him?

Hebrews 4:12 (NKJV) For the word of God is living and powerful, and sharper than any two-edged sword, piercing even to the division of soul and spirit, and of joints and marrow, and is a discerner of the thoughts and intents of the heart.

There is a danger in cognitive-behaviour theory because it is more oriented to the utility of an individual's belief than the truth. Rather than replace lies with truth, cognitive- behaviour therapy simply replaces unhelpful thoughts with helpful ones. This opens a wide range of the door to relativism, a doctrine that knowledge, truth, and morality exist in relation to culture, society, or historical context and are not absolute.

The cognitive-behaviour view of human nature is inaccurate. The theory is rooted in naturalism and therefore is not cognizant of the spiritual and does not accept the concept of God. In some ways, the cognitive-behaviour perspective alludes to the fact that human beings possess a sinful nature. However, it also advocates that humans are capable of self-salvation. We are not. Revising our thoughts will not save us.

At the same time, cognitive therapy's goal of self-acceptance is not inherently unbiblical. God accepts us in our imperfections. We obtain grace by faith, not by self-salvation or cognitive behavioural therapy detection.

Ephesians 2:1-10 (NKJV) And you, He made alive, who

were dead in trespasses and sins, in which you once walked according to the [a]course of this world, according to the prince of the power of the air, the spirit who now works in the sons of disobedience, among whom also we all once conducted ourselves in the lusts of our flesh, fulfilling the desires of the flesh and of the mind, and were by nature children of wrath, just as the others. But God, who is rich in mercy, because of His great love with which He loved us, even when we were dead in trespasses, made us alive together with Christ (by grace you have been saved), and raised us up together, and made us sit together in the heavenly places in Christ Jesus, that in the ages to come He might show the exceeding riches of His grace in His kindness toward us in Christ Jesus. For by grace you have been saved through faith, and that not of yourselves; it is the gift of God, not of works, lest anyone should boast. For we are His workmanship, created in Christ Jesus for good works, which God prepared beforehand that we should walk in them.

Colossians 2:13 (NKJV) And you, being dead in your trespasses and the uncircumcision of your flesh, He has made alive together with Him, having forgiven you all trespasses,

Romans 5:6-8 (NKJV) For when we were still without strength, [a]in due time Christ died for the ungodly. For scarcely for a righteous man will one die; yet perhaps for a good man someone would even dare to die. But God demonstrates His own love toward us, in that while we were still sinners, Christ died for us.

We are not left imperfect; Christ took our place and made us perfect. It is expedient to balance the truth of our justification with the process of sanctification. Cognitive behaviour therapy may have some attractions and helpful techniques for Christians seeking to take their thoughts captive or improve in other areas requiring self-control. It can also be beneficial in revealing the enemy's lies so that Christians are not duped into self-loathing, intense self-hatred, or self-defeating behaviours. However, to be free from false thoughts and mature as Christians, we need to be grounded in God's truth and sanctified by the power of the Holy Spirit. God's Word is powerful and sharp as a surgeon's scalpel, cutting through everything, whether doubt or defense, laying us open to listen and obey. Nothing and no one is impervious to God's Word. We can't get away from it—no matter what.

1 Peter 3:14-16 (NKJV) But even if you should suffer for righteousness sake, you are blessed. "And do not be afraid of their threats, nor be troubled." But [a]sanctify [b]the Lord God in your hearts, and always be ready to give a defense to everyone who asks you a reason for the hope that is in you, with meekness and fear; having a good conscience, that when they defame you as evildoers, those who revile your good conduct in Christ may be ashamed.

John 17:17-23 (NKJV) Sanctify[a] them by Your truth. Your word is truth. As You sent Me into the world, I also have sent them into the world. And for their sakes I sanctify Myself, that they also may be sanctified by the truth. "I do not pray for these alone, but also for those who [b]will believe in Me through their word; that they all may be one, as You, Father, are in Me, and I in You; that they also may be one in Us, that the world may believe that You sent Me. And the glory which You gave Me I have given them, that they may be one just as We are one: I in them, and You in Me; that they may be made perfect in one, and that the world may know that You have sent Me, and have loved them as You have loved Me.

Joshua 1:8 (NKJV) This Book of the Law shall not depart from your mouth, but you[a] shall meditate in it day and night, that you may observe to do according to all that is written in it. For then you will make your way prosperous, and then you will have good success.

John 8:32-33 (NKJV) And you shall know the truth, and the truth shall make you free."

Hebrews 4:12 (AMP) For the word of God is living and active and full of power [making it operative, energizing, and effective]. It is sharper than any two-edged [a]sword, penetrating as far as the division of the [b]soul and spirit [the completeness of a person], and of both joints and marrow [the deepest parts of our nature], exposing and judging the very thoughts and intentions of the heart.

CHAPTER 9

THE WINNER'S BRAIN

Psalm 139:14 (NKJV) I will praise You, for I am fearfully and wonderfully made; Marvelous are Your works, And that my soul knows very well.

Do not allow your fear, panic, or complex be greater than your purpose. You cannot manifest the wonderfully and fearfully made in you when ruled by fear, which is the antithesis of faith. Fear comes into your life only to downsize the original that is you. You need a lifestyle not determined by conditions and people but by God.

Your model and lifestyle should be when conditions through life go low; your spirit goes high. Your spirit is the one that should be in control during crisis; your body is addicted to your comfort zone and is always weak during a crisis.

Our greatest enemy is not the devil or Satan; our greatest enemy is ignorance. Because of fear and lack of knowledge, too many people dwindle and die, carrying seeds of greatness, unrealized potentialities, and undiscovered breakthroughs. Do not get trapped by the paralysis of your analysis. Your life can only go in the direction your mind is willing to transport it. It is only a matter of your will.

God created a human being that no adversity can incubate. Winning in life has little to do with your IQ, circumstances, financial resources, or luck.

But it has everything to do with creating a failure-resistant brain. You are specially made for nobody else but God. When you discover your chemistry, you will look for giants in your life to kill.

Every time you think, feel an emotion, or execute a behaviour, your Neurocircuitry (any mechanism that regulates neural activity) changes. The good news is that you can take charge of your process. The beauty is that everyone has what it takes to succeed simply because everyone has a brain. You can transform your thinking, emotions, behaviour, and even your physical structure so your brain can reach its full potential.

The average brain does a pretty good job of getting by daily. It has over one hundred billion brain cells serviced by a super-highway of blood vessels to help you think your thoughts, move your body, and experience the world around you, acting with speed and efficiency that most advanced computers cannot rival.

Resilience (the ability to recover quickly from every difficulty or toughness) and motivation are two of the critical abilities for which winners' brains are wired and conditioned. You will win through every toughness; you must have these two abilities.

The winner's brain operates differently than the average brain. When you reorient your brain's processing power, it helps to perform better despite interruptions. This process is called focus reinvestment. The winner's brain fires up the motivation to push through boredom while the brains of less tenacious individuals seem to run out of steam.

Improve your thinking to improve your life. Every time you think a thought, feel an emotion, or execute a behaviour, there is always a corresponding change within your brain. If your reaction is positive, your brain will react positively, and if it is negative, it will respond negatively. Your life is a product of your thoughts and behaviour. You can unlock the door and consciously, deliberately, and successfully control much of your brain's switchboard to better position yourself to achieve your goals and dreams.

The brain is active and subject to change no matter what you do; this is a key discovery of modern neuroscience. What sets the owner of a winner's brain apart is the desire and the know-how to take charge of their process. What you are going through parallels with what God is doing and has done in your life. You only need to discover yourself.

How you think and behave will affect your brain, and changes in your brain can, in turn, further affect your thoughts and behaviour. I dispel the myth that achievers are all born hardwired for success and that you are either born with a high-functioning brain or not. We know that the brain changes based on what its owner chooses to do with it. Take the reins and nurture the nature you have. Even into old age, we can adapt our brains. The brain retains a capacity for change until the day you die.

There are endless opportunities for improvement, and when you actively take charge of how your brain works, you have a better chance of influencing your fortunes. Nobody blows your trumpet if you don't yourself. Do not question those who tried and failed but question those who failed to try.

1 Timothy 6:12 (NKJV) <u>Fight the good fight</u> of faith, lay hold on eternal life, to which you were also called and have confessed the good confession in the presence of many witnesses.

We all know that no fight in the natural is good. The fight is a struggle that involves fear and pain, emotions, etc., but in the supernatural, fight is good because it brings out the brilliance in you. Life is a fight; you will fight loneliness, sicknesses, diseases, poverty, depression, mindsets, attitudes and behaviours, lifestyle, marriage, single life, family, workplace, and everywhere. There is a fight to fight. The good news is when you discover how capable you are of fighting; you go around looking and searching for the giants in your life to kill.

Develop a ready resilience and maturity that you need to pick yourself up and remain standing, dust yourself up, keep moving through pain, and keep moving forward.

Suppose you are going to do something extraordinary. It takes courage. Courage to stand firm despite failure, opposition, and ridicule. Never allow yourself to be made a victim of someone's insecurity. Accept no one's proclamation and prediction that you are not good enough. Your test and trials cannot kill you only when you permit them. Your test preludes your next higher level and ground.

1 John 4:4 (AMP) Little children (believers, dear ones), you are of God and you belong to Him and have [already] overcome them [the agents of the antichrist]; because He who is in you is greater than he (Satan) who is in the world [of sinful mankind].

CHAPTER 10

SELF-CONSCIOUSNESS

Acts 19:15 (NKJV) And the evil spirit answered and said, "Jesus I know, and Paul I know; but who are you?"

Self-Consciousness is full awareness of oneself, your potential, actions, appearance, and intention. It is a conscious raising of one's state of belonging or originating in oneself. It is absolutely an intense awareness of who you are.

Finding who you are is a journey of self-discovery. Your identity isn't found in your name, beauty, degree, position, profession, accolades, family tree, or inheritance. Identity is not a definition.

Job 32:8 (NKJV) But there is a spirit in man, And the breath of the Almighty gives him understanding.

God expressed himself in you. He voice-printed you; your DNA has been voice-printed. God intends that you can express yourself in the world, in your region, in your environment, in your crisis and troubles; you have the potential to express yourself. God designs you to operate in dominion and live within the parameters of the law of aerodynamics "what goes up stays up." You have access to multiplication, dominion, and rulership to subdue every confrontation, regional or environment. Dominion does not mean arrogance or bullying people but staying in charge over life circumstances despite all odds.

The human being is triune. You are a spirit; you have a soul, and your body houses both your spirit and soul.

Genesis 2:7 (NKJV) And the Lord God formed man of the dust of the ground, and breathed into his nostrils the breath of life; and man became a living being.

You cannot define yourself based on the physical body. God gives you prudence through His Word to go through life journey or circumstances and definition. God's breath of life in you makes you a living soul, giving you the ability of perceptivity. You can perceive, be sensitive to occurrences, discerning in nature, and observant.

Loneliness is not the absence of people but the absence of purpose. When you find your purpose, the people will come, but you become desolated when you waste your purpose in life. Most times, people define you based on your outward manifestation, but the people in question do not have access to know who you are. Relationships define you, make you happy, feel you are wanted and cherished, or belittle and downplay who you are. Jesus Christ withdrew Himself from the people who do not know Him.

Most of the time, we give people access to be the engine of our definition, our worth, our decision making, our life compass or navigator, and we end up not maximizing our God-given potentialities. Your soul is responsible for your identity; if the enemy can control your soul, He can control your identity, and external forces will control your life and circumstances.

If you are rejected because you chose to be you, not manipulated by eternal forces or anybody, rejection is not a sign that something is wrong with you. Rejection is a divine announcement that the person who rejected you has no longer the capacity for your greatness because you are impregnated with divine purposes that no human has control over. Stop asking the permission of people to be just who you are. Don't waste your experiences. You are designed not to waste your spiritual and divine experiences, don't waste yourself, don't waste your life trying to be who God has not made you to be.

The problem is that your environment has picked up so many mental viruses, lies, and stereotypes about you that are contrary to God's vision. You need to come in the volume of what is written—God's revelation of you.

Matthew 4:7 (NKJV) Jesus said to him, "It is written again, 'You shall not tempt the Lord your God.'

You need to develop "It is Written Mentality" over circumstances and people who come into your life only to downsize who you are. Every problem that comes into your life is a test of your potential. God moves through the crisis in your life. Crisis is a divine announcement that God is ready for your abundant outpouring and wants you to move to a higher dimension.

People who are a product of their environment behave and function like the environment they live in and trade their identity to embrace what their environment offers.

Genesis 1:26 (NKJV) Then God said, "Let Us make man in Our image, according to Our likeness; let them have dominion over the fish of the sea, over the birds of the air, and over the cattle, over all the earth and over every creeping thing that creeps on the earth."

That you are created in the IMAGE OF GOD means you have dominion, and to have dominion means to operate in higher frequencies even in an environment of low esteem that you must function in higher frequencies. God gave you the capability to function on higher frequencies irrespective of what confronts you consistently. You must subdue and exercise dominion, which you cannot do if you are not undaunted. Be aware that there is a pharaoh in your exodus whose consciousness is not to let you go.

When your identity is in crisis, you will have a low frequency to function, and that is when you make such confession that downsizes your dynamics "I am sick," "I have depression," "I am weak and poor," "I don't have luck," "I think I am under demonic influence," "I am jobless," "I am sad," "I am broke." All such statements come when your frequencies are low in function. The devil takes advantage during such times, knowing you have lost who you are in such a situation -THE IMAGE OF GOD.

Proverbs 6:2 (NKJV) You are snared by the words of your mouth; You are taken by the words of your mouth.

Proverbs 23:7a (NKJV) For as he thinks in his heart, so is he.

God reveals Himself to you at the speed of thought, and the devil also reveals himself and seduces you at the speed of thought and auto-suggestion.

Hebrews 4:16 (NKJV) Let us therefore come boldly to the throne of grace, that we may obtain mercy and find grace to help in time of need.

CHAPTER 11

SPLIT THE SEA SO I CAN WALK ON

Man is the driver of his destiny through his choices and vocabulary. The Image of God in you can become astronomically infinitesimal through the negative words you speak. A Christian's crucial evidence of truth is in how he uses and chooses vocabulary. With words, we make love and crush hearts. With words, we build faith and build fear in our lives and that of men.

Proverbs 11:9 (NKJV) The hypocrite with his mouth destroys his neighbor, But through knowledge the righteous will be delivered.

It is perfect practice that makes perfect, not practice that makes perfect.

If you know the Word, there will be a difference. As faith

comes to you, don't just agree by mental assent; respond by confessing the same things; soon enough, you will change the situation. Build your faith with the Word of God. As you study, your heart is flooded with wisdom and spiritual understanding, not just to know but also to walk in your destinies.

Discover the elite, uniqueness, and treasures within by towering your life with positive words, the right choice, perceptions, and the right way of thinking. What you do with your words will determine what your words will do with you.

Your words have creative ability, power, and energy both in positive and negative directions. Think the truth, peace, success, and love before you speak

Matthew 22:29 (NKJV) Jesus answered and said to them, "You are mistaken, not knowing the Scriptures nor the power of God.

When people lack accurate and relevant spiritual information from God's Word, they experience defeat and failure. Ignorance can cause you to be a defeated Christian.

Psalm 82:5-7 (NKJV) They do not know, nor do they understand; They walk about in darkness;

All the foundations of the earth are unstable.

I said, "You are gods. And all of you are children of the

Most High. But you shall die like men, And fall like one of the princes.

Psalm 82:5-7 describes the debacle and despondency of the one who is ignorant of his heritage and identity. What is the problem? Ignorance, they know not, neither do they understand; they walk on in the darkness, destroyed by sickness elements, and plummeted by the harsh elements of this world.

The Word of God is your teacher; if you look at your teacher, you will never fail. The voice speaking governs authority. God uses the intensity of the crisis in your life and the force of adversity to rid us of the impurities that lead to mediocrity.

Divine brilliance is the more you overcome, the more valuable you ultimately become. Each challenge you face is a divine invitation for you to gain clarity concerning who you are and why you are here.

Diamond originated from the Greek word "Adamas," meaning unconquerable, unalterable, and unbreakable. You are a diamond in the rough; life's complications strengthen your credibility and build your capacity. Problems will shine divine spotlights on hidden possibilities that have been dormant. As the diamond is a natural resource to the earthly man, you are a supernatural resource to God.

Every challenge is an adventure. Don't hyperventilate or advertise your problems because nobody will buy them, face them with divine weapons. If you expose your fear, you bury your talent. Bury your fear to be able to apprehend your talent.

A man's thoughts, if wrongly employed, can keep him in bondage and clog the wheels of his success and progress. Your life will never be different from the character of your thoughts.

John 11:39 (NKJV) Jesus said, "Take away the stone." Martha, the sister of him who was dead, said to Him, "Lord, by this time, there is a stench, for he has been dead four days."

Most of us have become uncomfortable with our complications and situations. When the Lord God calls to roll the stone, we are bent on complaining about how much our situation stinks when divine intervention is waiting at our door. Jesus is the resurrection, and He is passionate enough to resurrect your complications and troubles. Roll away the stone of your situation and stop hyperventilating about how much it stinks. We are concentrated on what stinks and neglect the reality of the resurrection.

Child of God, you are a rainbow. A rainbow is a witness of divine faithfulness and a sign of the covenant. You are so colourful to God. When you have big things to do and a world to take, you cannot afford to focus on frivolities and mundanities- impatient and lacking seriousness or silly and being secular or worldly.

Your words are your servant. This is not the time to mountain-climb, but a time to speak to your mountain; your weapon is unorthodox, watch your words, or they become your destiny.

CHAPTER 12

DIVINE POWER/AUTHORITY IS A LOGICAL CONSTRUCT

The Spirit of the resurrected Christ Jesus takes up residence in a believer in Christ. The Holy Spirit begins to govern the individual, giving the gift of self-control or self-government. The believer in Christ has been anointed and appointed under the auspices of the Holy Spirit for action, to live for purpose and objectivity.

Acts 1:8 But you will receive power when the Holy Spirit comes on you; and you will be my witnesses in Jerusalem, and in all Judea and Samaria, and to the ends of the earth."

The hallmark of the charismatic church is to manifest the power of God on earth. To exercise God's power, you must eliminate the intimidation factor, which is unbelief. The power is to change a believer to conform to the image and ability of God through his action in demonstrating the Word of God and using the Name of Jesus Christ.

Mark 16:17-18 And these signs will accompany those who believe: In my name they will drive out demons; they will speak in new tongues; they will pick up snakes with their hands; and when they drink deadly poison, it will not hurt them at all; they will place their hands on sick people, and they will get well."

Power is a logical construct referring to various ideas relating to ability and capacity. Power comes from the ancient Greek word Dunamis, portrayed as a significant cosmic principle.

Romans 1:16 For I am not ashamed of the gospel, because it is <u>the power of God</u> that brings salvation to everyone who believes: first to the Jew, then to the Gentile.

The Power highlighted here in Romans 1:16 renders the Greek word Dunamis, which means that the Gospel is the dynamite of God. The English word dynamite is derived from the Greek word Dunamis. The Gospel of our Lord Jesus is the dynamic power of God conveyed through God's message when presented to the world; the Gospel dynamically works salvation in those who believe.

2 Peter 1:3 His divine power has given us everything we need for a godly life<u> through our knowledge of him</u> who called us by his own glory and goodness.

For you to have and experience the power of God, you must

know Him, the power of God is not given to a stranger; your money cannot buy it like Simon the sorcerer thought he could receive power by giving money to the Apostles Peter and John. Acts 8:18-19 And when Simon saw that through the laying on of the apostles' hands the Holy Spirit was given, he offered them money, saying, "Give me this power also, that anyone on whom I lay hands may receive the Holy Spirit."

Philippians 3:10 that I may know Him and <u>the power of His resurrection,</u> and the fellowship of His sufferings, being conformed to His death,

Luke 24:49 I am going to send you what my Father has promised; but stay in the city until you have been <u>clothed with power from on high</u>."

The believer is empowered divinely; the context views this power as channeled through knowledge and virtue. Apostle Peter did not consider this power passive but the foundation and motivation to pursue a circle of virtues. The person Who possesses the characteristic of power is the Prime Mover of the universe. Therefore, this God brings the world into existence and distributes power to people to fulfil His historical purposes.

Jeremiah 27:5 <u>With my great power</u> and outstretched arm I made the earth and its people and the animals that are on it, <u>and I give it to anyone I please.</u>

Jeremiah 32:17 Ah, Sovereign Lord, you have made the heavens and the earth by <u>your great power</u> and outstretched arm. Nothing is too hard for you.

Power is an inherent characteristic of God; it results from God's Nature. God's kind of power is seen in His creation.

Deuteronomy 3:24 "Sovereign Lord, you have begun to show to your <u>servant your greatness</u> and your strong hand. For what god is there in heaven or on earth who can do the deeds and mighty works you do?

Romans 1:20 For since the creation of the world, God's invisible qualities—<u>his eternal power and divine nature</u>— have been clearly seen, being understood from what has been made, <u>so that people are without excuse.</u>

Power is always a derived characteristic for people who receive power from God. When humans perceive their power as intrinsic to themselves, they are self-deceived.

Deuteronomy 8:17-18 You may say to yourself, "My power and the strength of my hands have produced this wealth for me." But remember the Lord your God, for it is he who gives you the ability to produce wealth, and so confirms his covenant, which he swore to your ancestors, as it is today.

Jesus as God in Flesh demonstrated the intrinsic and derived aspects of power from the Father.

John 5:27 And he has given him authority to judge because he is the Son of Man.

John 17:2 For you granted him authority over all people that he might give eternal life to all those you have given him.

Jesus also demonstrated that His power was derived from His authority as the Son of man and that the two were an inseparable testimony to His divine nature.

Power without authority is not productive. It is like taking an examination without results. God delegates particular authority to particular people to minister His grace and truth in this world. Power is given to be exercised, and the action in exercising or the doing of power is the authority. God's calling in our lives depends on our responses, "Here am I send me Lord" the most incredible peace, prosperity, joy, fulfilment, self-esteem, etc., come from participating in God's work and vineyard. You do what the Giver of power says you should do with it, and when you do, you have acted on the authority that created the power. We have the authority to use and demonstrate the Word of God and the authority to use the name of Jesus. (2 Corinthians 4:20, Psalm 107:20, Colossians 3:17). He sent His Word and healed their diseases.

John 14:12 Very truly I tell you, whoever believes in me will do the works I have been doing, and they will do even greater things than these, because I am going to the Father.

Jesus gave the seventy-two disciples the authority to trample on snakes and scorpions. The issue facing contemporary Christian is how God exercises His authority in the spiritual realm that is the Church. God exercises authority over the Church through His Word, imparting authoritative truth.

The Bible issues definitive directives; it offers an authoritative norm by which all doctrine and principles must be shaped for individual believers and the church. The Bible chronicles an explanation of divine revelation that is complete, sufficient, and comprehensible for salvation. The source of authority from a Christian perspective is the Bible. This is the most important source of authority for Christians as it contains the teachings of God and Jesus Christ.

Isaiah 55:11 So shall My word be that goes forth from My mouth;

It shall not return to Me [a]void, But it shall accomplish what I please,

And it shall prosper in the thing for which I sent it.

Matthew 28:18 Then Jesus came to them and said, "All authority in heaven and on earth has been given to me.

Luke 10:18-19 And He said to them, "I saw Satan fall like lightning from heaven. Behold, I give you the authority to trample on serpents and scorpions, and over all the power of the enemy, and nothing shall by any means hurt you.

The concept of authority refers to the ability or capability to complete an action- Jesus was given authority by God. Authority is the tenacity to direct actions or thoughts. It is the power of attorney or right to issue commands and punish violations, usually because of rank or office. Authority comes from the Greek word exousia, which is the ability or strength with which an individual is endued, which he either possesses or exercises and uses to extinguish every onslaught of adversity. It is an influence or privilege, the power of judicial decisions, the legitimacy which grants and justifies the right to exercise the power of God.

The term power identifies the ability to accomplish an authorised goal of compliance or obedience. Hence authority is the power to make decisions and the legitimacy to make such legal decisions and order their execution. Authority is the freedom to decide or a right to act without hindrance; all authority begins with God.

Romans 13:1 Let every soul be subject to the governing authorities. For there is no authority except from God, and the authorities that exist are appointed by God.

The authority is valueless without the power to make it effective; we can make a fine distinction between the two concepts. This first understanding of authority is distinct from power and refers primarily to a prerogative. The concept of authority refers to the ability or capability to complete an action. Jesus was given the authority to forgive sins.

Matthew 9:6 But that you may know that the Son of Man has power on earth to forgive sins.

The word authority is used in reference to delegated authority in the form of a warrant, license, or authorisation to perform. Jesus was asked

by whose authority He taught. Matthew 21:23 Now, when He came into the temple, the chief priests and the elders of the people confronted Him as He was teaching, and said, "By what authority are You doing these things? And who gave You this authority?"

Jesus was granted authority for His ministry by His Father

John 10:18 No one takes it from Me, but I lay it down of Myself. I have power to lay it down, and I have power to take it again. This command I have received from My Father."

Believers have the right to become children of God

John 1:12 But as many as received Him, to them He gave the [a]right to become children of God, to those who believe in His name:

God gave the apostles license to build the Church. 2 Corinthians 10:8 For even if I should boast somewhat more about our authority, which the Lord gave [a]us for [b]edification and not for your destruction, I shall not be ashamed—

The natural extension of power, meaning exousia, sometimes

denotes the sphere in which authority is exercised. God has established spheres of authority worldwide, such as civil government.

Authority is used to protect the rights to life, liberty, and prosperity, provide order and security in people's lives - traffic controllers (evil has its traffic), prevent accidents, and provide safety for airplane passengers protection. Authority can be used to manage conflict.

The question of authority from a theological perspective is the most significant of all the approaches. It is a fundamental issue facing every person, especially the believer. Its significance cannot be overestimated. Everyone has authority in life that they submit to as a subordinate, not by constraints but by conviction.

Furthermore, God created human beings to live under His authority. They sin when they choose to live under a different rule, that of self or an idol. In a simple summary, this is the teaching of Genesis 3:1: Now the serpent was more cunning than any beast of the field which the Lord God had made. And he said to the woman, "Has God indeed said, 'You shall not eat of every tree of the garden?'"

This portion of the Scripture illustrates the human tendency, moved by pride, to seek independence from external authority and establish self as the final authority in life. God exercises His authority over creation and His creatures. God has established three fundamental spheres of authority, family, the Church, and the state within which He delegates authority to an individual believer.

Romans 8:19 For [even the whole] creation [all nature] waits eagerly for the children of God to be revealed.

Matthew 4:19-20 Then He said to them, "Follow Me, and I will make you fishers of men." They immediately left their nets and followed Him.

The making power of God is in following and knowing Him; you cannot be fishers of men without revealing the resurrection power of Christ in your life and your tenacity and zeal to demonstrate the power through the authority of the Word of God and the name of Jesus. All you need is to follow Jesus Christ. Only Him can transform. There came a time in Apostle Peter's life when he did not follow Christ with his whole heart; he followed afar off.

Matthew 26:58 But Peter followed him at a distance, right up to the courtyard of the high priest. He entered and sat down with the guards to see the outcome.

At the same time, we cannot be clothed with the world and Christ and expect God's dynamic power at its climax or epic. Following Christ, afar off or from a distance, places a believer in the place of natural operation. Apostle Peter follows afar off, leaving the position of power and fishers of men and returning to his regular fishing duties. Following Christ from a distance makes a believer in Christ vulnerable to backsliding and puts him in a place of self. You need greatness and power, love Christ more. The power of God can always be obtained from the upper room. Every believer in Christ can create their upper room where the power of God is available and efficacious. When the power of God comes on you, you can release your spiritual DNA to the world around you, and God confirms His Word.

Hebrews 2:3-4: how shall we escape if we neglect so great a salvation, which at the first began to be spoken by the Lord, and was confirmed to us by those who heard Him, 4 God also bearing witness both with signs and wonders, with various miracles, and gifts[a] of the Holy Spirit, according to His own will? (NKJV).

The hallmark of the Church is the compelling charm that inspires devotion to exercising the power of God in others. It was the power in action, the authority to demonstrate the Word of God. The power is the unity between God and us. Jesus came to show us God's idea- people. Most people in the world don't read the Bible; they read us; it is expedient that we live by the power of the resurrected Christ.

Acts 19:20 So mightily grew the word of God and prevailed.

Believers in Christ should crave the principles of succeeding in being anointed and appointed. We should believe in the redemptive power of Christ and understand God's dream is to reproduce Himself in us.

Ephesians 1:17-18 [I always pray] that the God of our Lord Jesus Christ, the Father of glory, may grant you a spirit of wisdom and of revelation [that gives you a deep and personal and intimate insight] into the true knowledge of Him [for we know the Father through the Son]. And [I pray] that the eyes of your heart [the very center and core of your being] may be enlightened [flooded with light by the Holy Spirit], so that you will know and cherish the [a]hope [the divine guarantee, the confident expectation] to which He has called you, the riches of His glorious inheritance in the [b]saints (God's people),

We should be identified with Christ, *Hebrews 12:2 looking unto Jesus, the [a]author and [b]finisher of our faith, who for the joy that was set before Him endured the cross, despising the shame, and has sat down at the right hand of the throne of God. (NKJV)*

Colossians 1:25-27 I have become its servant by the commission God gave me to present to you the word of God in its fullness— the mystery that has been kept hidden for ages and generations but is now disclosed to the Lord's people. To them God has chosen to make known among the Gentiles the glorious riches of this mystery, which is Christ in you, the hope of glory.

We should live the love of Christ

1 Corinthians 13:1-4 &13 If I speak in the tongues[a] of men or of angels, but do not have love, I am only a resounding gong or a clanging cymbal. If I have the gift of prophecy and can fathom all mysteries and all knowledge, and if I have a faith that can move mountains, but do not have love, I am nothing. If I give all I possess to the poor and give over my body to hardship that I may boast, [b] but do not have love, I gain nothing.

Love is patient, love is kind. It does not envy, it does not boast, it is not proud. 13 And now these three remain: faith, hope and love. But the greatest of these is love.

John 4:8 Whoever does not love does not know God, because God is love.

We should all participate in building God's Church; we must understand that the lowest person if there is any, is created in the image of God. Jesus sent us to the world to reveal Him. Jesus lived to self-breath anyone who believes in Him.

2 Corinthians 6:4-10 Rather, as servants of God, we commend ourselves in every way: in great endurance; in troubles, hardships and distresses; in beatings, imprisonments and riots; in hard work, sleepless nights and hunger; in purity, understanding, patience and kindness; in the Holy Spirit and in sincere love; 7 in truthful speech and in the power of God; with weapons of righteousness in the right hand and in the left; through glory and dishonor, bad report and good report; genuine, yet regarded as impostors; known, yet regarded as unknown; dying, and yet we live on; beaten, and yet not killed; sorrowful, yet always rejoicing; poor, yet making many rich; having nothing, and yet possessing everything.

Mark 10:45 For even the Son of Man did not come to be served, but to serve, and to give his life as a ransom for many."

CHAPTER 13

WHAT YOU SPEAK LOCATES WHO YOU ARE

Matthew 12:34, CSB: Brood of vipers! How can you speak good things when you are evil? For the mouth speaks from the overflow of the heart.

The concept of identity and how identity is constructed is not new in sociolinguistic studies. It is commonly accepted that we shape our identity through spoken words and interactions with others. All interactions and discussions include the negotiation of identity in which speakers claim certain, assigned, discarded, and re-imagined identities in various ways- what you think and speak locates who you are, what you are, and what you intend to become. How you think, speak, and behave will affect your brain, and changes in your brain can, in turn, further affect your thoughts, and what you think controls your behaviour.

Proverbs 23:7 (AMP) For as he thinks in his heart, so is he [in behaviour—one who manipulates].

One of the unique gifts that God has given to us is the human mind. The ability to learn, think, choose, and reason is the essence of what makes us human. While the ability to think makes us human, it goes deeper. Your thoughts become a reflection of who you are. God certainly understands this, and he speaks to this in various places throughout his word.

How sensitive are we in speaking positively or negatively when faced with conundrums of life? When you *believe* what's in the heart, the thoughts, and inclinations of the heart shape the reality of who you are. They shape your thinking which will ultimately shape your actions.

The core of who you are is evidenced by the thoughts or roots of your heart. That's why what is on the inside is so important than what is on the outside. You can mask the outside to others, trying to bury it in the world around you. But, ultimately, what's in your heart will reveal who you are.

Proverbs 4:23 (NIV) Keep thy heart with all diligence, for out of it are the out-flowings of life.

There is not enough time to stop and think about what you want to say before speaking. We must instead learn spiritual principles to deal with the spiritual problem.

Your heart is the most important leadership tool you have. It is not your experience, knowledge, or skills. It is your heart that matters most of all. Likewise, if your heart is unhealthy, it impacts everything else. It threatens your family, friends, ministry, career, and legacy. It is, therefore, imperative that you guard it. The enemy uses all kinds of weapons to attack our hearts. These attacks often come in the form of circumstances that lead to disappointment, discouragement, or even disillusionment. In these situations, one is tempted to quit—to walk off the field and surrender.

Many Christians suffer from obesity, hypertension, and depression at higher rates in the last decade, their use of antidepressants has risen, while their life expectancy has fallen.

Our words either empower or contradict our confession. The average person speaks 18000 to 25000 words daily, a 54-page book daily, or 66800 pages a year. Women averagely speak more words than men in a day. The difference in daily word count between men and women has a biological orientation. It results from hormone differences in men and women, which is the major contributor. Women have significantly different hormone makeup than men do.

Additionally, there are slight but noticeable differences in brain structure between men and women. On average, girls learn to speak before boys. Generally, they tend to have better language development in early childhood, coupled with biological differences with social norms and gender stereotypes (men are supposed to be stoic and endure pain or hardship without showing feelings or complaining).

The Greek word "glossa" means tongue or language- the mouth's organ of taste and speech.

God created the universe by His Word, and He assumes humanity should be established through spoken words and will be known by their words. God assumes there will be a connection between His Word, which created the universe, and human words, which should result from their divine providence. Hence, any faith that does not transform the tongue is no saving faith.

God made humanity freelance beings and gave them the right to make their choices. Your tongue and your choices decide your destiny. Your tongue can bury and burn or build up and exalt your life. Our words can contradict our confessions. The control of the tongue is an indicator of our maturity, and it locates who masters or is in control. Our words can create a great future or cause a significant conflict lifelong.

Your tongue can either write your destiny to success or write your destiny to destruction. The human tongue has enormous potential for blessings and condemnation; the tongue is either a choice promoter or a choice killer. The focal point of our rise and fall and depravity is the mouth. The mouth is the monitor of the human condition.

Right words will build righteous life, and bad words will build a fallen life of misery. We will be negative people if we get negative talk flowing from our mouths. If we let worrisome talk proceed from our mouths, we become worried people; if we speak sadly, we become sad; if we speak bitter words, we become bitter; if we gossip, we become gossips, etc. Words are used for blessing and cursing.

Psalm 45:1 (KJV) My heart is indicting a good matter: I speak of things which I have made touching the king: my tongue is the pen of a ready writer.

Proverbs 18:20-21 (NKJV) A man's stomach shall be satisfied from the fruit of his mouth; From the produce of his lips he shall be filled. Death and life are in the power of the tongue, And those who love it will eat its fruit.

Words are powerful living things and are biological, negative, or positive in growth. They give us the power to heal and the power to hurt. Power to give hope and discourage, the power to build up and tear down. No family, friendship, marriage, or relationship isn't made more robust or weaker by how you choose and use your words.

James 3:2-12 (NKJV) For we all stumble in many things. If anyone does not stumble in word, he is a perfect man, able also to bridle the whole body. Indeed, we put bits in horses' mouths that they may obey us, and we turn their whole body. Look also at ships: although they are so large and are driven by fierce winds, they are turned by a very small rudder wherever the pilot desires. Even so the tongue is a little member and boasts great things. See how great a forest a little fire kindles! And the tongue is a fire, a world of iniquity.

Words are powerful living things and are biologically negative or positive in growth. They give us the power to heal and the power to hurt. Power to give hope and to discourage, the power to build up and tear down. There is no family, friendship, marriage, or relationship that isn't made stronger or weaker by how you choose and use your words.

In a rigorous tongue analysis, the book of James, chapter 3 is a veritable pathology laboratory in which analysis and diagnosis occur. The mature person can bridle his tongue. The person who does this is a master of the whole body. Interactive effects of self-esteem, contingencies of self-worth and ego, threat on supportiveness and liking, targets high or low in self-esteem and evaluative feedback, interpersonal appraisals, and adverse effects of individualism on interpersonal relationships and happiness are all the products of spoken words.

The nurse puts a thermometer under your tongue and tells your physical temperature. According to the book of James, the tongue also determines your spiritual thermometer. The mouth or the tongue does not operate independently of any other impulse. They are the organs by which the heart expresses itself. The mouth is a living symbol of what is in your heart.

Psalm 141:3 (AMP) Set a guard, O Lord, over my mouth; Keep watch over the door of my lips [to keep me from speaking thoughtlessly].

Your tongue can create and destroy, it has the potential to call the impossible into being, and it can close doors of your future. Depending on how you use your tongue, the negative directions will produce negative results, and a positive reflection will yield positive results. Your tongue can create and destroy, it has the potential to call the impossible into being, and it can close doors of your future. Depending on how you use your tongue, the negative directions will produce negative results, and a positive reflection will yield positive results.

Matthew 12:36-37 (NKJV) But I say to you that for every idle word men may speak, they will give account of it in the day of judgment. For by your words you will be justified, and by your words you will be condemned."

James 1:19 (NIV) My dear brothers and sisters, take note of this: Everyone should be quick to listen, slow to speak and slow to become angry,

Psalm 141:3 (AMP) Set a guard, O Lord, over my mouth; Keep watch over the door of my lips [to keep me from speaking thoughtlessly].

Proverbs 6:2 (NKJV) You are snared by the words of your mouth; You are taken by the words of your mouth.

Unregenerate tongue roams wildly to defend itself, quick to attack others,

Proverbs 15:28 (NKJV) The heart of the righteous studies how to answer but the mouth of the wicked pours out evil things.

You can unlock the door and consciously, deliberately, and successfully control much of your tongue switchboard to better position yourself to achieve your goals and dreams. Whenever you think low and negative, your brain reacts low by allowing your tongue to talk low; in antithesis, when your thoughts are high, your brain reacts to let your tongue bring out your brilliance.

Matthew 18:18 (NIV) "Truly I tell you, whatever you bind on earth will be[a] bound in heaven, and whatever you loose on earth will be[b] loosed in heaven.

The pinnacle of the truth leads you to a place of sovereignty, of dominion, a place where any situation cannot move you. You have a fixed position in Christ's stead because of the authority of the Word of God to bind, loose, and set free with the efficacy and potency of God's Word in your mouth.

Jeremiah 5:14 (NIV): Therefore this is what the Lord God Almighty says: "Because the people have spoken these words, I will make my words in your mouth a fire and these people the wood it consumes.

Philemon vs6 (NKJV) that the sharing of your faith may become effective by the acknowledgment of every good thing, which is in you in Christ Jesus.

What you are going through is parallel with what your tongue has spoken. With your tongue and your choices, you can create a failure-resistant life. Don't allow your fear, panic, and nervousness to be greater than your purpose. Know your purpose and keep it.

Romans 10:10 For with the heart one believes unto righteousness, and with the mouth confession is made unto salvation.

Your thoughts should fire up your motivation to talk positive and push you tenaciously through boredom. Less tenacious individuals seem to talk themselves low and easily run out of steam. Change your thinking to improve your life. Every time you think, speak a word, feel an emotion, or execute a behaviour, there is a corresponding change within your brain. The Word of God must be stored in your heart and spoken; it must go forth to be accomplished; it must be spoken into a situation to become Rhema- Spoken Word and must prosper and materialize.

Isaiah 55:11 (NKJV) So shall My word be that goes forth from My mouth; It shall not return to Me [a]void, But it shall accomplish what I please, And it shall prosper in the thing for which I sent it.

Difficulty rises and brings perplexity because we do not see God as more significant than all. Observance comes from an inward holy flame kindled by the Holy Spirit.

Hebrews 4:12 (NKJV) For the word of God *is* living and powerful, and sharper than any two-edged sword, piercing even to the division of soul and spirit, and of joints and marrow, and is a discerner of the thoughts and intents of the heart.

CHAPTER 14

APPYLING THE LAW OF GRAVITY AND AERODYNAMICS IN THE SUPERNATURAL

The Law of Gravity states anything that goes up must indeed come down, while the Law of aerodynamics states that it is possible that something can go up and remain there.

The plan of God is not for us consistently go up and down but to maintain staying up in prosperity because nothing can cause and dethrone what and who God has blessed.

Proverbs 23:18 (NIV) There is surely a future hope for you, and your hope will not be cut off.

Jeremiah 29:11-12 (NIV) For I know the plans I have for you," declares the Lord, "plans to prosper you and not to harm you, plans to give you hope and a future. Then you will call on me and come and pray to me, and I will listen to you.

The law of aerodynamics has always been present, even before it was understood and used enough to develop airplanes for flight. Whether it is the law of aerodynamics, Moses, or Isaac Newton, every law was placed there by God to teach us the truth about our reality.

Colossians 1:16-17 (NIV) For in him all things were created: things in heaven and on earth, visible and invisible, whether thrones or powers or rulers or authorities; all things have been created through him and for him. He is before all things, and in him all things hold together.

We understand through science and the Word of God how the Law of Aerodynamics, which is the law of the Spirit of Life, and the Law of Gravity, which is the law of sin and death, operate. Before a plane takes off and builds momentum, it lifts off the ground and begins to soar. While the airplane is building momentum, the law of Gravity is actively present and persistently trying to keep the aircraft on the ground. But another superior law is applied that lifts the plane off the ground and pulls it upwards, defying the law of Gravity-the Law of Aerodynamics.

This same application is reminiscent of Apostle Paul's writings in

Romans 7:22-23 (NIV) For in my inner being I delight in God's law; but I see another law at work in me, waging war against the law of my mind and making me a prisoner of the

law of sin at work within me.

The Law of sin and death was always present. The Law of Gravity or sin and death was introduced due to the fall of man. In ourselves, we cannot overcome the Law of sin and death. It takes a higher and greater law to free us from the bondage of sin and death, which is the law of the Spirit of life in Christ Jesus. The law of the Spirit of life is known as the Law of Grace.

Romans 7:25 (NIV) Thanks be to God, who delivers me through Jesus Christ our Lord! So then, I myself in my mind am a slave to God's law, but in my sinful nature[a] a slave to the law of sin.

Romans 8:2 (NIV) because through Christ Jesus the law of the Spirit who gives life has set you[a] free from the law of sin and death.

It is only in Christ that the law of Sin and death is broken, and His grace is sufficient for us.

Philippians 3:9-11 (NKJV) and be found in Him, not having my own righteousness, which is from the law, but that which is through faith in Christ, the righteousness which is from God by faith; that I may know Him and the power of His resurrection, and the fellowship of His sufferings, being conformed to His death, if, by any means, I may attain[a] to the resurrection from the dead.

If the laws of Aerodynamics are applied, Gravity has lost its hold, and the plane can break free from the bonds of the earth as it lifts itself 35000 feet above the earth's atmosphere. We are a type of aircraft called, created, and chosen in Christ from the foundation of the world. We entered a realm we thought was our real world and saw ourselves as human beings separated from God. Because of this mindset, the law of Gravity or sin and death worked against us, pulling us down and keeping us in the confines of the earthly realm. When you work in sync to understand your life is hidden with Christ in God, and you are one with the Father, Gravity loses its hold, and you are propelled into heavenly places, breaking the law of Gravity.

Galatians 5:25 (NKJV) If we live in the Spirit, let us also walk in the Spirit.

If we live by the Spirit, if we derive our life from the Spirit, if it is by the action of the Spirit that our moral activity as Christians is alive and orchestrated. If we are indeed endued with the quickening Spirit, Who causes us to die to sin and alive to God. Let us show it in our deals.

Victorious living and effective soul-winning service are not the product of our better selves and hard endeavors but are simply the fruit of the Holy Spirit. We are not called upon to produce the fruit but to bear it. It is all the time to be Christ's fruit. Nothing is more expedient than we should be continuously filled with the Holy Spirit or keep to the metaphor that the trees of Christ should be constantly full of His strength.

CHAPTER 15

LONELINESS IS NOT ALONENESS

Genesis 2:18 (NIV) The Lord God said, "It is not good for the man to be alone. I will make a helper suitable for him."

Humans are social species that require safe and secure social surroundings to survive. Satisfying social relationships are essential for mental and physical well beings.

Loneliness can be conceived as a social deficiency. Loneliness exists to the extent that a person's network of social relationships is smaller or less satisfying than a person desires. Although loneliness is not only a result of less crowd around, but you can also still be with a crowd and feel lonely; you can be with your spouse, family, children, and friends and feel lonely. When your life has a spiritual void, you can be in a crowd and feel extremely lonely.

Conventional measurement techniques can ascertain a person's desired or preferred level of social contact. Loneliness is not synonymous with aloneness, social isolation, or solitude. Aloneness is being apart from others, solitary, being without anyone, or considered separately from all others exclusively; aloneness emphasizes one's desire to be alone at specific times for social, professional, spiritual, personal, etc. Aloneness is not loneliness; it is physical isolation that is self-imposed. I am not lonely, but I am alone working. "Jesus is an example of One Who preferred aloneness for communion with the Father God. He continually withdrew from people, daily life activities, and the demands of His ministry to be alone with the Father and pray; solitude and silence are significant themes in the Gospel.

Luke 5:16 (NIV) But Jesus often withdrew to lonely places and prayed.

Mark 1:12 (NIV) At once the Spirit sent him.

Mark 1:35 (NIV) Very early in the morning, while it was still dark, Jesus got up, left the house and went off to a solitary place, where he prayed.

Matthew 14:23 (NIV) After he had dismissed them, he went up on a mountainside by himself to pray. Later that night, he was there alone..

Daniel and John were all in a solitary place to receive the vision of God

Daniel 10:8 (NIV) So I was left alone, gazing at this great vision; I had no strength left, my face turned deathly pale and I was helpless.

Revelation 1:9 (NIV) I, John, your brother and companion in the suffering and kingdom and patient endurance that are ours in Jesus, was on the island of Patmos because of the word of God and the testimony of Jesus.

Loneliness is perceived as a global human phenomenon. The feeling of loneliness or being detached from others is not just a human emotion; it is a complex emotional response to the lack of companionship. Loneliness is a state of mind that causes people to feel empty, alone, unwanted, and isolated. Lonely people crave contact. One in every five people globally is lonely, and a majority don't have somebody to talk to or spend time with, and this rate is increasing rapidly due to high technology.

The manifestation of loneliness can be divided into cognitive, motivational, and behavioural. Loneliness is an emotionally unpleasant experience linked with feelings of general dissatisfaction, unhappiness, chronic depression, anxiety, emptiness, boredom, restlessness, and marginality. With modernization, loneliness has increased since people are engrossed in virtual social communities and networks and don't have the urge to attend social gatherings or stay in touch with family and friends. These make people vulnerable, affect physical and mental health, and increase mental health disorders. Loneliness is a universal human emotion that is complex and unique to everyone. Loneliness has no common cause; it has many adverse effects on physical and mental health, including depression and suicide, cardiovascular diseases, and stroke.

The state of mind makes it more difficult to form connections with people. Loneliness is not only an absence of people but a state of mind. You can be with a crowd and still feel lonely, your family, friends, and loved ones, and still feel lonely. From a case study of experts, loneliness is not expedient about being alone; instead, if you feel alone and isolated, that is how loneliness plays into your state of mind.

Loneliness is strongly connected to genetics; other contributing factors include situational variables, such as physical isolation, moving to a new location, and divorce. The death of a loved and significant one, loss of a job, mobbing, situational child development like growing up with unaffectionate or over critical parent may make an individual shy away from intimacy with others, communication handicap with peers, over aggressive or demanding personalities, make people withdraw from social situations they believe will lead to rejection. Loneliness can be a lifestyle for those who struggle with poorly developed interpersonal skills. Social factors like technology rob people of the time to be with others. It can be a symptom of a psychological disorder such as depression. Loneliness can also be attributed to internal factors such as low self-esteem and lack of confidence. The feeling of unworthiness, needing attention, or not being regarded by people can lead to depression and chronic loneliness.

Loneliness triggers health-associated risks and diseases such as depression and suicide, cardiovascular disease, and stroke, increases stress levels, decreases memory and learning ability, triggers anti-social behaviour, increases poor decision-making, the risk of alcoholism and drug abuse, and the progression of Alzheimer's and alters brain functions. Lonely adults become vulnerable to consuming more alcohol and get less exercise than those who are not lonely.

The diet of lonely folks is higher in fat, they sleep less efficiently, and they report more daytime fatigue, constantly tired during the day because of sleepless nights. Loneliness also disrupts the regulation of cellular processes deep within the body, predisposing people to age quickly. Loneliness increases high blood pressure, high cholesterol, and obesity. It increases the concentration of cortisol levels in the body, and prolonged elevated cortisol levels can cause anxiety, depression, digestive problems, heart disease, sleep problems, and weight gain. Case-study of older adults and social isolation concluded that those without adequate social interaction were twice as likely to die prematurely. Loneliness promotes short-term self-preservation, including an increased implicit vigilance for social threats; in contrast to non-social threats, loneliness is a serious health risk.

Social Isolation can exacerbate a person's feelings of low

esteem, low self-worth, shame, loneliness, depression, and other mental concerns. Loneliness may be contagious. Researchers examined how loneliness spreads in social networks in a ten-year case study. The result indicated that people close to someone experiencing chronic loneliness were 52% more likely to become lonely.

You can transform loneliness; you cannot fight with darkness or loneliness and fear of isolation directly; the reason is that all these mentioned do not exist. They are absolutely and simply an absence of something, just as darkness is the absence of light. How do you bring light into dark places? You just switch on the light. Loneliness can be overcome. It requires a conscious effort on your part to make a change. Changing in the long term can make you happier and healthier and enable you to impact others around you positively. Your burden triggers a miracle; your burden sets you up for a miracle. Your burden is not a generational curse but a setup for the manifestation of God's glory.

Admit the problem; when you acknowledge that you are lonely, you can take the necessary steps to escape your situation. Consider the causes and evaluate your life honestly in light of the factors, why you got into a place of loneliness, what caused your loneliness, and how you can escape. Accept what cannot be changed, the death of a spouse or loved one, a relocation away from old friends, and other unalterable circumstances must be faced squarely. Recognize that loneliness is a sign that something needs a change in you, understand the effects that loneliness has on your life both physically and mentally, and consider doing community service or another activity that you enjoy that presents opportunities to meet people and cultivate new friendships and social interaction, focus on developing quality relationships with people who share similar attitudes, interest, and values with you and expect the best.

Lonely people often expect rejection, so instead, focus on positive thoughts, train your vocabulary to be positive, and create new positive attitudes and values within yourself. Reposition yourself to be the positive and extraordinary driver of your destiny. Develop new habits that build up your inner self; as you become stronger and more self-assured, you will find it easier to make new friends and confront new situations. Exercise regularly, take long walks, and go to the gym to feel physically and emotionally fit. Establish a schedule for very day, weekend, or week. Loneliness seems intense when we have nothing to do and no plan. Organize your time to include some outside activities. Practice looking at yourself from God's perspective irrespective of human definitions and tags on you. Study the Scriptures and meditate on the verses that depict God's view of His Children.

We have an innate need to be loved and belong by God's design. From childhood, we learn to give and receive affection and are taught the skills that will help us find acceptance in God and humanity. We form our sense of individuality and find our place in divinity through our relationships with God, family, friends, co-workers, and others. When that need for affection and fellowship goes unfulfilled, we become empty, restless, and unhappily lonely.

Psalm 68:5-6 (NIV) A father to the fatherless, a defender of widows, is God in his holy dwelling. <u>God sets the lonely in families</u>,[a] he leads out the prisoners with singing; but the rebellious live in a sun-scorched land.

The spiritual loneliness of being separated from God creates an empty vacuum and can only be filled by God Himself; it is a deep need calling into deep. Christians who attend church and do not get involved in Church activities cut themselves off from a rich source of companionship. In the cases of spiritual loneliness, the crowd and human relationships cannot fill in the gap until God comes in. We need to connect with something more significant than ourselves to fill the spiritual void. The Bible is God's plan for developing most relationships in our lives. The Bible highlights one preeminent relationship from God's point of view. That is the fellowship He wants to have with us, forming the foundation of all other relationships. When we accept God's gift of salvation or eternal life through Jesus Christ, we enter communion with the Creator of the universe. God Almighty becomes our heavenly Father and places His Spirit within us. Jesus referred to the Holy Spirit as the Counsellor.

John 14:16 (NIV) And I will ask the Father, and he will give you another advocate to help you and be with you forever—

God's Spirit fills believers with the assurance of our membership in God's family. Daily, through prayer and Bible reading, we can experience the wonderful fellowship God wants to have with His Children. He is never too busy to listen. A dynamic walk with God is a solid foundation for building relationships with others. As God's children, our brothers and sisters inhabit every nation on the globe. Spiritually speaking, our immediate family is the group of believers with whom we attend Church. They form an essential support group that functions much more beyond the natural family. If you are a Christian suffering loneliness, ask yourself if you fully possess the abundant life God wants you to have. Have you confessed Christ as your Saviour? Making Jesus Christ the Lord of your life will put you on a path that leads to intimacy with God, new friendships with fellow Christians in this life, and an eternal place in God's presence in the life hereafter.

John 14:6 (NIV) Jesus answered, "I am the way and the truth and the life. No one comes to the Father except through me.

Psalm 16:11 (NIV) You make known to me the path of life; you will fill me with joy in your presence, with eternal pleasures at your right hand.

Hebrews 12:22-29 (NIV) But you have come to Mount Zion, to the city of the living God, the heavenly Jerusalem. You have come to thousands upon thousands of angels in joyful assembly, to the church of the firstborn, whose names are written in heaven. You have come to God, the Judge of all, to the spirits of the righteous made perfect, 24 to Jesus the mediator of a new covenant, and to the sprinkled blood that speaks a better word than the blood of Abel. See to it that you do not refuse him who speaks. If they did not escape when they refused him who warned them on earth, how much less will we if we turn away from him who warns us from heaven? At that time, his voice shook the earth, but now he has promised, "Once more, I will shake not only the earth but also the heavens." [a] The words "once more" indicate the removing of what can be shaken—that is, created things—so that what cannot be shaken may remain. Therefore, since we are receiving a kingdom that cannot be shaken, let us be thankful, and so worship God acceptably with reverence and awe, 29 for our "God is a consuming fire." [b]

Engage in an ongoing work process on yourself and spend more time developing yourself. You never realize your greatness when you become sidetracked by secondary activities. Living is complicated; life is challenging. You will never have a problem-free moment in life. Don't spread yourself tin; write the script of your life. You can learn all the technics in the world; if you don't believe in yourself, it will come to nothing. Courage means going from failure to failure without losing enthusiasm or energy. To start God's desire for your life is to amass weight; you can become your gargantuan self if you desire.

CHAPTER 16

TRANSFORMATION IS INTERNAL

Proverbs 16:27 (NKJV) An ungodly man digs up evil, And it is on his lips like a burning fire.

You can call yourself a Christian and still be ungodly; a carnal person is not someone who does know God but one who lives his life on the five senses, whose mind is not subject to renewal and transformation. He is controlled and remote-controlled by the flesh or the body and his environment.

Romans 12:2 (NIV) Do not conform to the pattern of this world, but be transformed by the renewing of your mind. Then you will be able to test and approve what God's will is—his good, pleasing and perfect will.

When the mind is transformed, the person will be changed as well. The reason is the war zone, the battlefield where every war is fought and won. Wilderness living is a state of existence when nothing positive grows in your life, living an unproductive life and existence. One of the causes of wilderness living is jealousy, envy, and comparing oneself with others. Wrong thought patterns won't get us blessed; God has an individual plan for each of us. Be honest with God about your feelings. If the enemy can hide in your soul, he will always have a certain amount of control over you.

Every moment we make a proclamation or an announcement that Jesus is the answer, we need to ask ourselves what the question is? You cannot proclaim an answer when there is no question. For every cause, there is a cost, but we are not dealing with the cost; we should confront the cause. Any mature religion must start questioning itself and conducting a reality check. It is in questioning yourself that you begin to grow up. In questioning yourself, you discover your fallow grounds and master areas that need change.

Romans 8:5 (NIV) Those who live according to the flesh have their minds set on what the flesh desires; but those who live in accordance with the Spirit have their minds set on what the Spirit desires.

In infancy, when we were young, we believed and accepted everything; in maturity, we must question everything and choose what we accept. That song that says, "give me that old-time religion," is wrong; we are in trouble because old-time religion had less commitment and education; many became indoctrinated to church rules and regulations, not indoctrinated to the unadulterated Christ and His Word.

John 1:3-5 (NIV) Through him all things were made; without him nothing was made that has been made. In him was life, and that life was the light of all mankind. The light shines in the darkness, and the darkness has not overcome[a] it.

As Christians, let us ask, is miracle something external or internal? Physical demonstrations can happen externally, but not until your heart changes and there is an ongoing renewal; there is no miracle. A miracle is an internal manifestation.

And many of us want to see apparitional miracles or supernatural appearances, manifestations, or phantoms. We want to see fire out of the mouth and men falling. We want apostles out of cellphones and iPads. The real miracle is "The things I used to do; I do them no more, the places I used to go, I go there no more, the person I used to be, I am no more, the song I used to sing, I sing them no more "there is a significant change since I was born again. "

If you want to look for a miracle, look for internal work of grace, not an external demonstration of an act. Miracle starts inside out. Miracle dwells in the place of the inner man. Until the internal changes, the external cannot change; that's where Christians are getting it wrong. Internal does not offer them a comfort zone. A disciplined nature orchestrates every change of internal. Some people will never like you because your spirit irritates their demons. Their demons cannot fathom the supernatural Entity living in your spirit, man.

Although the Bible warns of attitudes and activities to stay away from, how seriously do most Christians follow biblical counsel? God's cautions are for our good and health; ignoring His guidance and commands opens us to being misled. The fire has no dominion over you if you live in the supernatural.

Daniel 3:16-18 (NIV) Shadrach, Meshach and Abednego replied to him, "King Nebuchadnezzar, we do not need to defend ourselves before you in this matter. If we are thrown into the blazing furnace, the God we serve is able to deliver us from it, and he will deliver us[a] from Your Majesty's hand. But even if he does not, we want you to know, Your Majesty, that we will not serve your gods or worship the image of gold you have set up."

The fire of life does not burn a transformed mind, those who live in the supernatural daily. Every prophetic Word of God demands your personal engagement. To have prophetic dominion in every area of our endeavors, we need a changed heart and a transformed mind. The quality of your faith is not measured in your comfort zone where there is no trial.

Isaiah 43:2,4, 10 (NIV) When you pass through the waters, I will be with you; and when you pass through the rivers, they will not sweep over you. When you walk through the fire, you will not be burned; the flames will not set you ablaze. Since you are precious and honoured in my sight, and because I love you, I will give people in exchange for you, nations in exchange for your life. Lead out those who have eyes but are blind, who have ears but are deaf. You are my witnesses," declares the Lord, "and my servant whom I have chosen, so that you may know and believe me and understand that I am he. Before me, no god was formed nor will there be one after me.

Colossians 2:6-8 (NKJV) As you therefore have received Christ Jesus the Lord, so walk in Him, rooted and built up in Him and established in the faith, as you have been taught, abounding [a]in it with thanksgiving. Beware lest anyone [b] cheat you through philosophy and empty deceit, according to the tradition of men, according to the basic principles of the world, and not according to Christ.

1 Corinthians 15:58 (NIV) Therefore, my dear brothers and sisters, stand firm. Let nothing move you. Always give yourselves fully to the work of the Lord, because you know that your labor in the Lord is not in vain.

CHAPTER 17

UNDERSTANDING DIVINE PROGRESSION

Progression is a protocol or a process of developing or shifting gradually towards a more advanced level or state—the exigent demands of life demand progression. We should try to clear the phantoms from our heads and grasps divine realities. We should be full of incandescent love for God, His Word, our lives, and the lives of others. The most profound devotion is based on a personal relationship with God and humanity hence love the Lord your God and your neighbour as yourself. This is the hallmark of progression.

Romans 2:1-4 (NKJV) Therefore you are inexcusable, O man, whoever you are who judge, for in whatever you judge another you condemn yourself; for you who judge practice the same things. But we know that the judgment of God is according to truth against those who practice such things. And do you think this, O man, you who judge those practicing such things, and doing the same, that you will escape the judgment of God? Or do you despise the riches of His goodness, forbearance, and longsuffering, not knowing that the goodness of God leads you to repentance?

Sometimes people try to put us out of progression by not seeing anything good in us; they try to quench the race of progression by condemning everything we do, everything we are, and everything we try to be. When you absorb the condemnation of people around you, it has the tenacity to put you out of your race and self-worth.

You are a person of destiny. Regardless of whatever you've been told, you are not a mistake. Each time you stand before God's mirror, what you see is reflected in the Glory of God. If your reflection is the Glory of God, then you are the Glory of God.

John 17:22 (NKJV) And the glory which You gave Me I have given them, that they may be one just as We are one:

The Glory is not a natural decoration; the Glory has been given to you as a believer in Christ Jesus to be God's representative on the everyday scene, especially today's scene. God acts in "the now." What matters right now is how God sees you, other people may not see you as the Glory of God, but God is mindful and sees you in the light that no other person can see.

Your life's journey begins with the word you speak and hear, positive or negative. Words have the potential to reverse any situation. You are called to make the Word of God your foundation; you can't build any solid life without God's Word as your foundation.

2 Corinthians 3:18 (NKJV) But we all, with unveiled face, beholding as in a mirror the glory of the Lord, are being transformed into the same image from glory to glory, just as by the Spirit of the Lord.

As we continually look into the Word, we discover new heights and ways and make progress. You discover who you are in the Word of God, and transformation into everything the Word of God says about you transpires.

Philippians 2:12 (NKJV) Therefore, my beloved, as you have always obeyed, not as in my presence only, but now much more in my absence, <u>work out your own salvation</u> with fear and trembling;

Salvation means preservation or deliverance from harm, ruin, or loss, from sin and its consequences through faith, redemption, help, saving, and reclamation. It would help if you were ox-minded about your salvation because nobody will carry your cross or work it out for you. Others may try for you, but you are still the navigator of your own life.

Proverbs 29:18a (KJV) Where there is no vision, the people perish:

Vision is ethereal, seeing something coming into view as if it were already there, visions are perceived and conceived first in the supernatural realm before they manifest in the material world or physical realm. Making progress without a vision can be dolorous or grievous.

There are three kinds of people in the world today-(a) Those who never seem to be aware that things are happening around them, (b) Those who ask, "what happened? (c) Those that make things happen.

The Book of Acts of the Apostles was called "Acts" because the Apostles were known for their acts, not their talk. They were doers. They were visionaries. Towns and cities became nervous when they showed up because of their doings and performances, not their talking. They were labeled "Men who turned the world upside down."

Acts 17:6 (NKJV) But when they did not find them, they dragged Jason and some brethren to the rulers of the city, crying out, "These who have turned the world upside down have come here too.

Change will always upset people who are content to be stagnant, but you should be known for your vision. It is depressing and frustrating to have an idea for years that you haven't yet cultivated or have come to pass.

The poorest person in the world is a person without a dream and purpose, and the most frustrated person in the world is someone with a dream and purpose but doesn't know how to bring it to pass. No matter how much money you may have, you are truly poor if you do not have a clear vision for your life. If you don't know where you are going, any road will take you there.

You must have a vision beyond your current circumstance. A visionless life is a poverty-stricken existence. An English adage says, "Where there is a will, there is a way." Vision is the primary motivator of human action. Vision influences the way you conduct your entire life. God has placed a vision in your heart to guide you; without vision, you will have no values in your life. Your vision is the key to fulfilling your life's purpose.

In economics, the value of something is determined by how rare it is. If you know your value today, things will go well for you tomorrow. It is depressing to be around people who just exist, but it is exciting to be around people who know they are doing what they were born to do. People don't fulfill their visions because they have no sense and perception of their destiny.

Let your purpose become your passion. Most people are interested in their destinies but have no desire or drive to fulfill them. Make your passion an antidote to depression; it will cause you to have joy amid significant opposition.

When God told Noah to build an ark and consulted many

people to help, he was mocked and laughed at, but Noah did not let distractions and mockery steal his vision or progression; he held on to the vision despite distractions.

When the flood came, God said to Noah in Genesis 7:1, "Go into the ark" Because Noah stayed in the ark, he never paid attention to the flood and the storm. When you hold on to your vision and remain in the ark (Lord Jesus), you will never notice the intensity of the floods, the storms, and the waves.

"The same flood that caused destructions was still the same that brought Noah's ark to rest on the Mountains of Ararat in Turkey." <u>Your vision will take you beyond your flood if you stay in Jesus, "He is the Ark."</u>

The same storms that disturb you will be the same storm that opens doors for your higher levels and supernatural promotions.

God has given every person a gift or talent for which the world will make room. The gift enables you to fulfil your vision. *Proverbs 17:8 says, "A gift is as a precious stone to the one who has it,"* And *2 Timothy 1:6 says, "For this reason, I remind you to fan into flame the gift of God which is in you."*

You stir up or fan to flame your gift by developing, refining, enhancing, and using it. This is where education comes into play. Education cannot give you gifts, but it can help develop your gifts. Education is not the key to success; otherwise, every Ph.D. holder should have been financially secure and happy. You will probably be poor if you are intelligent and not exercising your gift.

If you are educated but have not developed your talent, you will likely be depressed, frustrated, and tired. You will hate to go to work on Monday mornings. Some have degrees in finance and have hard times making ends meet. Doesn't it make you nervous when people with no money are trying to tell you how to make a million dollars when they don't have a cent?

Education is very imperative, but education itself doesn't guarantee anything. It is your gift that is the key to your success. You don't realize that the gift you are sitting on is loaded with potential for your higher levels. *Proverbs 18:16 says, "A man's gift brings him before great men."* Anyone who develops his gift will become a commodity in commerce. Michelangelo, Beethoven, and Bach died five hundred years ago, but their gifts are still alive in schools and speaking for them.

Louis Armstrong applied at a young age to go to music school. He was given scales to sing at the audition, but he could only sing the first two notes and was rejected. Still, he came out crying and telling his friends, "I know there's music in me, and they can't keep it out." He eventually became one of the most successful and beloved Jazz musicians of all time, sold records, made money, and won hall of fame accolades.

Louis knew he was an original and couldn't allow other voices to kill his vision and progression. Although we are born originals, most of us decide to become imitators and fake. You are created to stand out and not to bend in. To understand vision is to realize that it always emanates from purpose. God is the Author of and vision. It is His nature to be purposeful in everything. Every time God appeared on the scene in human history, it was to accomplish something purposeful in life. *Isaiah 14:24 says, The Lord Almighty has sworn surely as I have planned, so it will be and as I have purposed, so it will stand." Nothing can get in the way of God's purposes; they always come to pass.*

Ecclesiastes 3:10-12 (NIV) I have seen the burden God has laid on the human race. He has made everything beautiful in its time. He has also set eternity in the human heart; yet] no one can fathom what God has done from beginning to end. I know there is nothing better for people than to be happy and do good while they live.

"Burden" is a heavy responsibility, occupation, or task in Hebrew. It could be described as a responsible urge to carry out all that you were designed. There is eternity in the human heart. This is what the Bible meant by "deep calling unto deep" in *Psalms 42:7 "Deep calls to deep in the roar of your waterfalls; all your waves and breakers have swept over me."*

Don't be discouraged when others around you seem to be making more progress than you. God has a unique plan for your life, unlike any other living person. His purposes and plans for your life are unique; He doesn't have, has never had, and will never have a copy of you. This is why you are you: As long as the earth remains, you are the only one God will ever have. Take pride in your uniqueness and what God is doing in your life.

Don't measure your success or failure with someone else. It is how much you are walking in the will of God that determines your progress. Stop running another man's race; outdo your past and not another man's past. Aim high, faith acts in boldness and the now. Faith cannot postpone for tomorrow. You who say, "I will have faith tomorrow; faith is now." Except if you understand these principles, your life will be full of murmur. You begin to build the kind of life protection you need if you feel storms of life have battered and tattered you for so long.

CHAPTER 18

WHO IS A SAINT?

The human definition of a saint is motivated and driven by ignorant. They say a saint is a person officially recognized by canonization as capable of interceding for people on earth. A person who has died and gone to heaven, the likes of St. Agnes, Agatha, Ambrose, Patrick, Anthony, Theresa, Bartholomew, Basil, Benedict, Boniface, Catherine, Christopher, Cyril, Kelvin, etc.

The Bible says that the new creation is a saint; when you are born again, you are born into God's family not by merit but by grace, and you become a saint of God not because you are perfect but because your spirit is recreated.

Who is a saint? A Christian is a saint. A saint is a person sanctified, separated from God through the newborn experience. *2 Corinthians 5:17 "Therefore, if anyone is in*

Christ, he is a new creation; old things have passed away; behold, all things have become new" A saint is a holy or godly person, one who has been redeemed through the death of Christ on the cross. If you are a born-again Christian, you are a saint; that's your identity. The word saint is taken from the Hebrew word Hagios in Old Testament and Chaciyd in New Testament, meaning holy one, consecrated, separated, chosen by God, and separated for a divine purpose. Until you recognize "who you are," you cannot walk in the divine purpose for your life.

Psalms 16:3 But to the saints that are in the earth and to the excellent, in whom is all my delight.

2 Corinthians 8:4 Imploring us with much urgency that we would receive the gift and the fellowship of the ministering to saints.

Psalm 149:5 Let the saints be joyful in glory, let them sing aloud upon their beds vs6 let the high praise of God be in their mouth and a two-edged sword in their hands.

The dead cannot sing aloud, cannot be joyful, or handle a two-edged sword in their hands; in other words, dead folk cannot pray.

Colossians 1:26 Even the mystery which hath been hid from ages and from generations but now is made manifest to His Saints.

A dead person cannot receive revelation from God, revelation is for service, and a dead man cannot be called to service. God reveals only to saints who are alive so they can handle the onslaughts of the enemy. The devil is not interested in the dead but in the living to destroy their destiny and identity.

Acts 26:10, which thing I also did in Jerusalem and many of the saints did I shut up in prison, having received authority from the chief priest, and when they were put to death, I gave my voice against them.

There was no record that Saul put to death Christians in prison, but it is written that he persecuted Christians and saints who were in God's vineyard and killed many.

Romans 1:7, To all that, be in Rome, beloved of God called to be saints, Grace to you and peace from God our Father and the Lord Jesus Christ. The emphasis is on those who live in Rome, those who are still alive and well in Rome.

Philippians 4:22 All the saints salute you. If saints were dead believers, a dead person cannot salute or say hello to any.

Ephesians 6:18 Praying always with all prayer and supplication in the spirit and watching thereunto with all perseverance and supplication for all saints.

Praying for saints who are alive, not the dead ones; it is the living that needs enablement to overcome life circumstances.

Acts 9:32 &41 And it came to pass, as Peter passed throughout all quarters, he came down also to the saints which dwelt at Lydda. Vs41 And he gave her hand and lifted her up and when he had called the saints and widows presented her alive.

Peter went to living saints in Lydda, raised someone from the dead, and called in living saints to present the raised individual to them. Peter did not go to canonize dead saints.

Ephesians 2:19-20 Now therefore ye are no more strangers and foreigners but fellow citizens with the saints and of the household of God.

When you realize who you are and walk in the light of it, the devil and his cohorts will recognize your status in the Lord. Begin to see yourself as a saint of God; it is your inheritance as a born-again Christian. *Matthew 12:37, "For by your words you will be justified and by your words you will be condemned."*

Colossians 2:8-10 Beware lest anyone cheat you through philosophy and empty deceit, according to tradition of men, according to the basic principle of the world and not according to Christ vs9 For in Him dwells all the fullness of the Godhead bodily vs10 and you are complete in Him, who is the Head of all principality and power.

Hosea 4:6 my people are destroyed for lack of knowledge. Because you have rejected knowledge, I also will reject you from being priest for me. Because you have forgotten the law of your God, I also will forget your children.

Psalm 37:28 For the Lord loves justice and does not forsake His saints; they are preserved forever, but the descendants of the wicked shall be cut off.

Psalm 116:15 Precious in the sight of the Lord is the death of His saint. A saint is not one dead already.

Daniel 7:27 Then the kingdom and dominion, and the greatness of the kingdoms under the whole heaven shall be given to the people, the saints of the Most High. His kingdom is an everlasting kingdom, and all dominions shall serve and obey Him.

Romans 8:27 now He who searches the heart knows what the mind of the spirit is because He makes intercession for the saints according to the will of God.

The Holy Spirit makes intercession for the saints because He knows the will of God. It is not saint Ambrose, Mary the mother of Jesus, St Anthony, St. Theresa, or Patrick making intercession but the Holy Spirit.

1 Corinthians 1:2 To the Church of God which is at Corinth, to those who are sanctified in Christ Jesus, called to be saints, with all who in every place call on the name of Jesus Christ our Lord, both theirs and ours.

A saint is one who is sanctified and not one who is dead already because a dead man, the likes of St Ambrose, Anthony, and Patrick, cannot call on the name of Jesus Christ. *For in death there is no remembrance of you, in the grave who will give you thanks. (Psalm 6:5).*

There are a lot of other references (1 Corinthians 6:1-2, Revelation 20:9, Acts 9:13, Acts 26:10, Colossians 1:1, Philippians 4:21, Romans 16:2, Ephesians 4:11-12, Ephesians 5:3, Ephesians 1:1, 1 Samuel 2:9. Psalm 34:9, Revelation 13:7, Philippians 1:1).

A saint is one who, according to 2 Peter 1:1 Simon Peter, a bondservant and apostle of Jesus Christ, to those who have obtained like precious faith with us by the righteousness of our God and Savior Jesus Christ.

A SAINT IS NOT PERFECT:

Ephesians 4:11-12 And He Himself gave some to be apostles, some prophets, some evangelists and some pastors and teachers vs12 for the perfecting of the saints for the work of ministry, for the edifying of the body of Christ.

"For the perfecting and edification of the saints," meaning that the saints are not perfect people or the holy of all holies but people under the grace of God. They grow from glory to glory.

Romans 12:13 Distributing to the necessity of saints given to hospitality. Saints are people of God who are still alive and well and do have need to be met.

IGNORANT OPERATION THROUGH MEDIUM / FAMILIAR SPIRITS:

God the Father is the only one who has full supernatural power to answer any of our specific prayer requests through the name of Jesus Christ. A saint who has died and gone to heaven is not omnipresent; God is Omnipresent.

It is an act of divination to pray through saints who have died or pray through Mary, the mother of Jesus. *Colossians 3:17 And whatever you do in word or deed, do all in the name of the Lord Jesus, giving thanks to God the Father through Him.*

Deuteronomy 18:9 "When you come into the land which the Lord your God is giving you, you shall not learn to follow the abominations of those nations.

Leviticus 19:31 "Give no regard to mediums and familiar spirits; do not seek after them, to be defiled by them: I am the Lord your God.

Leviticus 20:6 "And the person who turns to mediums and familiar spirits, to prostitute himself with them, I will set my face against that person and cut him off from his people.

When you ask a dead man or woman to pray for you, you are engaging in the act of medium and familiar spirits.

1 Chronicles 10:13, so Saul died for his unfaithfulness which he had committed against the Lord, because he did not keep the word of the Lord and also because he consulted a medium for guidance. A saint is not a perfect person who does no wrong or does not have needs.

The devil, his cohorts, and the people he uses can demoralize your life by attacking your personality. When you are ignorant of your chemistry, the devil takes advantage and attacks your self-esteem. Somehow you begin to think you are worthless, just a good-for-nothing fellow, Mr. nobody. This experience was seen when the devil seduced Eve to lose her identity at the beginning of creation.

Genesis 3:2-5 And the woman said unto the serpent, We may eat of the fruit of the trees of the garden vs3, but of the fruit of the tree which is in the midst of the garden, God has said you shall not eat of it neither shall you touch it lest you die vs4 And the serpent said unto the woman you shall not surely die vs5 for God do know that in the day you eat thereof, then your eyes shall be opened and you shall be as gods, knowing good and evil.

The devil's purpose was to destroy Adam and Eve's identity and destiny. The devil's purpose for every human life is to assure that God's purpose for your life is ruined.

John 10:10 says The thief (devil) does not come except to steal and to kill and to destroy. I (Jesus Christ) have come that they may have life and that they may have it more abundantly.

Job 13:15 (NIV) Though he slay me, yet will I hope in him; I will surely defend my ways to his face.

1 Chronicles 10:13, so Saul died for his unfaithfulness which he had committed against the Lord, because he did not keep the word of the Lord and also because he consulted a medium for guidance. A saint is not a perfect person who does no wrong or does not have needs.

CHAPTER 19

LIVING THE VOLUME OF WHAT IS WRITTEN

Matthew 4:8-9 Again, the devil took Him up on an exceedingly high mountain and showed Him all the kingdoms of the world and their glory vs9 And he said to Him, "All these things I will give you if you will fall down and worship me."

The devil is always offering materiality to steal your identity and destiny.

Matthew 4:10 Then Jesus said to him "away with you, Satan, for it is written, you shall worship the Lord your God and Him only you shall serve"

Jesus came in the volume of what was written of Him. He knew His identity and destiny on earth and in heaven. He overcame the devil by exercising His dominion. You cannot defeat the onslaughts of the enemy without knowing who you are. The ugly circumstances of life confronting you will disappear when you come in the volume of what God has said about you. You must know that God created you to maximize your potential and purpose on earth.

Genesis 2:7 And the Lord God formed man of the dust of the ground and breathed into his nostrils the breath of life and man became a living soul.

God has given man everything he needed to function, but man has a choice to either exalt or limit himself. God created man with an extra potential as he breathed life into him, but man, being created as a freelance being, has the right to choose life that has the breath of God or death that has the devil's breath. Defeat does not exist in God's vocabulary. That's the reason He sees us as overcomers.

1 Corinthians 2:9-14 But as it is written, "eye has not seen, nor ear heard, nor have entered into the heart of man the things which God has prepared for those who love Him." But God has revealed them to us through His spirit. For the Spirit searches all things, yes, the deep things of God. For what man knows the things of a man except for the spirit of man which is in him? Even so, no one knows the things of God except the Spirit of God. Now we have received, not the spirit of the world but the spirit from God, that we might know the things that have been freely given to us by God. These things we also speak, not in words which man's wisdom teaches but which the Holy Spirit teaches, comparing spiritual things with spiritual. But the natural man does not receive the things of the spirit of God, for they are foolishness to him, nor can he know them because they are spiritually discerned.

2 Corinthians 8:9 For you know the grace of our Lord Jesus Christ, that though he was rich, yet for your sakes He became poor, that you through His poverty might become rich.

God gave man dominion so that man would become the compass of his life. Every authority has been made available to you, but authority cannot act itself unless you enforce it. Enforcing authority means you are acting it in words and attitude. God gives you His word to make you His word. Your destiny in the Spirit's realm is to be God's word. To effect changes by being a portrait of what the word says. Your nature and character is the word. The word of God is the ability you have, the word is Spirit, and they are Life. The energy and electricity that comes from your mouth is your ability to recreate your world.

Luke 10:19 "Behold I give you the authority to trample on serpents and scorpions and over all the power of the enemy and nothing shall by any means hurt you."

"Behold" is an emphasis that means "see" or "be conscious and understand." You have the choice to see or not see what ability has been made available for you. If you cannot see the ability, you cannot operate in the gravity of what is available. The authority is a power of attorney to act in Christ's stead.

Authority is acted and enforced by demonstration of power. If you have power and have not exercised authority, your power is a dead power. It is the authority that makes power meaningful. You may have power, but the power may be sleeping in you lifelong, but when you add authority to it, power becomes effective. Authority is dedicated, but power is inherited. Your words are backed up with power. They contain the inherent dynamic ability to cause changes in your circumstances.

1 John 4:17 Love has been perfected among us in this way, that we may have boldness in the Day of Judgment; because as He (Jesus) is, so are we in this word.

How was He? He went about doing good, healing the sick, and curing all sicknesses. He exercised the authority given to Him by the Father God in heaven. "As He is, so are we in this world. This means you have His ability, and His ability and authority you have are to be demonstrated.

There never is a day in your life that you have nothing, maybe ability, wisdom, authority, health, finance, etc. God never responded to needy people, but He responds to those who recognize their abilities and do exploits. Lions move by instinct. A Christian should be moved by the Holy Ghost. Your reward is decided by the kind of problem you are solving. Your ability will enable you to identify your identity. Trials are soils in which faith is planted. Afflictions and trials are a test of your identity, but they test you, and they don't break you. You cannot identify who you are if you have only good days; hallelujah and hosanna shout is not only when things are going good, it should also be applied in tested times when things are rough.

CHAPTER 20

CALLED TO BE AMBASSADORS

Isaiah 18:1-2 Woe to the land shadowed with buzzing wings, which is beyond the rivers of Ethiopia vs2 which sends ambassadors by sea, even in vessels of reed on the waters, saying "Go swift messengers, to a nation tall and smooth of skin. To a people terrible from their beginning onward, a nation powerful and trading, down whose land the rivers divide.

In the natural, an embassy is a building containing the offices of an ambassador and staff of diplomatic representatives, a place where ambassadors meet, a diplomatic center where policies and mandates are communicated, and a place of debriefing. In a place where ambassadors receive diplomatic immunity, we are heaven's ambassadors on earth. The church is our kingdom embassy.

You are an Ambassador for God here on earth. You are God's representative; anyone who confronts you confronts the one who sent you as a representative. Anyone who fights you fights God. We all know there is no foreign intervention in the premises of an Ambassador representing his country; such will jeopardize that country's sovereignty and raise tendencies to go to war. If there is an onslaught against you, it is an onslaught against God. The almighty God is mighty in battle; who can battle with the Lord? None can battle with the Lord.

Isaiah 54:17 says No weapon formed against you shall prosper, and every tongue which rises against you in judgment, you shall condemn. This is the heritage of the servants of the Lord, and their righteousness is from Me, says the Lord.

2 Corinthians 5:19-21: That is that God was in Christ reconciling the world to Himself, not imputing their trespasses to them and has committed to us the word of reconciliation vs20 Now then, we are ambassadors for Christ as though God were pleading through us; we implore you on Christ's behalf, be reconciled to God. For He made Him sin who knew no sin to be sin for us that we might become the righteousness of God in Him.

Ephesians 6:20 For which I am an ambassador in chains; that in it I may speak boldly as I ought to speak.

Your calling is to effect changes on earth in your life and

environment. Decree and declare kingdom purpose and allow God's plan to manifest through you. To uproot every darkness and plant light and life, to banish every presence of the enemy and opposition, to preach God's message to generations, and proclaim the acceptable year of the Lord.

Isaiah 61:1 The Spirit of the Lord is upon me, because the Lord has anointed Me to preach good tidings to the poor, He has sent me to heal the brokenhearted, To proclaim liberty to the captives, And the opening of the prison to those who are bound.

As an ambassador, you have identification in the Great Commission. You are called to represent God on earth. Your calling is a part of your identity. What are you called to do? What are you called for? Your purpose is in your identity. Have you discovered why you are planted here on earth? You are not here by accident; you didn't just happen, you are not a happenstance or a passerby. God called you to effect changes, to represent His purpose on earth.

Matthew 28:18-20 And Jesus came and spoke to them saying, "All authority has been given to me in heaven and on earth. "Go therefore and make disciples of all the nations, baptizing them in the name of the father and of the Son and of the Holy Ghost, "teaching them to observe all things that I have commanded you; and lo, I am with you always, even to the end of age."

Mark 16:15-18 And He said to them, "Go into all the world and preach the gospel to every creature. "He who believes and is baptized will be saved, but he who does not believe will be condemned. "And these signs will follow those who believe, In My name, they will cast out demons; they will speak with new tongues; they will take up serpents, and if they drink anything deadly, it will by no means hurt them; they will lay hands on the sick, and they will recover."

Your identity reflects who you are and what you are called to do in *1 John 4:7b, which says as Christ is on earth, so are we in this world. Christ lived and worked the calling of the great commission. He preached the gospel, healed the sick, and performed miracles. If you are as Christ is in this world, then your identity should be in line with his identity, and your works should be in line with His works on earth. Paul worked the work; that's why he was bold to say in Romans.*

Romans 1:16-17, "For I am not ashamed of the gospel of Christ for it is the power of God to salvation for everyone who believes, for the Jew first and also for the Greek. For in it, the righteousness of God is revealed from faith to faith: as it is written, "The just shall live by faith."

Being conscious of souls and saving them is why you are placed here as an ambassador and representative of Christ. Listen to what Paul says in Romans 11:14: "If by any means I may provoke to jealousy those who are my flesh and save some of them."

Live your identity to provoke jealousy for those who have not known Christ so that you can save them and win them to Christ through the manifestation of the Christ-like nature in you. Your identity must testify how good God is. There must be material and physical manifestations of God's goodness in you. The manifestation and testimony of what God has done in you and through you will provoke the unsaved to come to God through you.

Zechariah 8:23 "Thus says the Lord of hosts; In those days ten men from every language of the nations shall grasp the sleeve of a Jewish man, saying, 'Let us go with you, for we have heard that God is with you.'" (New King James)

Revelation 12:11 and they overcame him by the blood of the lamb and by the word of their testimony and they did not love their lives to death.

Matthew 10:27 "Whatever I tell you in the dark, speak in the light; and what you hear in the ear, preach on the housetops. (New King James)

UNLIMITED ACCESS:

Society may want to limit you, your family background, the nation where you live or come from, your education, job description, business, sickness, finance, friends, and gossip. There is a life that protects you from being limited, the daily life in Jesus Christ through the Holy Spirit. This life is organic, a life that propels your identity to operate in a higher subconscious, divine frequency and keeps your identity immune from onslaughts and penetrations of the enemy because of the breath of life in you and your regenerated spirit. If you have God, you have God's deluge of blessing upon your soul.

Your Identity is void of any human or devilish curse. *Numbers 23:8 says, "How can I curse those whom the Lord has not cursed? How can I denounce those who the Lord has not denounced? (NIV). Nobody has the authority to limit you or belittle you until you allow or give your permission. Sickness cannot even creep into your body until you let it; the breath of life in you cannot dwell side by side with illness.*

Hebrews 2:14-15: Inasmuch then as the children have partaken of the flesh and blood. He Himself likewise shared in the same that through death, He might destroy him who had the power of death that is the devil and released those who through fear of death were all their lifetime subject to bondage. (New King James)

We are called to exhibit and walk-in overcomer's consciousness that nothing can limit us except ourselves and ignorance. James 1:18 says, "Of His own will He brought us forth by the word of truth, that we might be a kind of first fruits of His creatures."

You are one of a kind in your identity.

You are what your vision is. If your vision is a winner's vision, you become a winner, but if your vision is a loser's, you become a loser. You are created a spiritual being for blessings because you are Abraham's seed.

Galatians 3:29 And if you are Christ's, then you are Abraham's seed and heirs according to the promise.

Zechariah 8:23 "Thus says the Lord of Hosts: In those days ten men from every language of the nations shall grasp the sleeve of a Jewish man, saying, "Let us go with you, for we have heard that God is with you."

You are a spiritual Jew. There is always something better for you, a more significant and higher level of success. Therefore, refuse the status quo and press on in victory. It does not matter how glorious your faith journey has been; there is always something better for you in Christ. All you need do is open your spiritual eyes to see the greater glory that lies ahead. This is where fellowship with the word and the Holy Spirit is indispensable.

GOD'S GLORY IN YOU:

You are a person of destiny regardless of whatever you have been told; you are not a mistake. Each time you stand before God's mirror, what reflects is the glory of God. If your reflection is the glory of God, then you are the glory of God.

John 17:22 And the glory which you gave Me I have given them, that they may be one just as we are one.

God's glory is not for decoration; the glory has been given to you to reflect it on everyday scenes, especially today's scene. The reason is that God acts in the now. God does not postpone His glory to reflect tomorrow; His glory is in the now. So, what matters now is how God sees you. Other people may not see you as the glory of God, but God sees you in a light that no other person can. When we have the right attitude, faith becomes remarkably active. But it can never be remarkably active in a dead life. Faith must bring evidence.

There is a place or an attitude (I think the word here should be altitude since we are talking of place) where God gives us faith to rest upon His word, and we delight inwardly over everything. It is the call of God that counts. Paul was in the call of God.

Acts 19:11-12, "Now God worked unusual miracles by the hands of Paul, so that even handkerchiefs or aprons were brought from his body to the sick and the diseases left them and the evil spirits went out of them."

It is the call of God that counts. Paul was in the call of God. *Acts 19:15 "Jesus I know, Paul I know but who are you" There must be a resemblance between you and Jesus. The evil spirit said, "Jesus, I know, and Paul I know, but who are you? Paul had a resemblance to Jesus. You cannot get this resemblance without having His presence. His presence changes you. You will not be able to get the results without the marks of the Lord Jesus Christ. The exorcists have no marks of Christ, so the manifestation of the power of Christ was not seen.*

If you want power, don't mistake speaking in tongues for power; if God has given you revelations along certain lines, don't mistake that for power, or if you have even laid hands on the sick and they have been healed, don't mistake that for power. *"The Spirit of the Lord is upon me because He has anointed me" (Luke 4:18); that alone is the power. Don't be deceived. God wants you to be ministering spirits, and this means being clothed with another power. The baptism of Jesus must bring you to the place of focusing on the glory of God. Everything else is a wasted time and wasted energy.*

Acts 9:6 "Lord, what do You want me to do"? This is the plan, and it means a perfect surrender to the call of God and perfect obedience. God has to take your tongue, thoughts, and everything you have, only Christ working through you.

To be baptized in the Holy Spirit is to be in God's plan, the Spirit preeminent, revealing the Christ of God, making the Word of God alive and something always divine.

2 Corinthians 3:5-6 Not that we are sufficient of ourselves to think of anything as being from ourselves, but our sufficiency is from God who also made us sufficient as ministers of the new covenant, not of the letter but of the Spirit, for the letter kills but the Spirit gives life.

In the regeneration process, you are being made like God, brought into the operation of the Spirit's power, and made like Him having His DNA. Your life becomes emblematic of Him. God wants us to come to a place where we will never look back. God has no room for those who look back, think, or act back. The rising tide is a changing of faith; it is an attitude of the spirit, where God rises higher and highest. Many people are missing God's highest order. It is a place our attitudes become altitudes.

May the Lord save the Pentecost experience from going to dry rot. Deliver us from any line of sentimentality, anything void of reality. We must be in a transforming position, not in a conforming condition, constantly renewing the mind, continually renovated by mighty thoughts of God. The depths of God come in with lowliness and meekness and cause the heart to love. No heart can love like the heart that God has touched. When the meekness and lowliness of the mind take hold, the preacher is moved by his Creator to speak from heart to heart and move people into the realm of the Spirit. You are created to rise into association with God in the Spirit. Never try to get the applause of people by any natural thing; yours is a spiritual work with a spiritual breath. The natural man decays, and you cannot do what you like with it. But the supernatural man may so abound in the natural man that it never decays. It can be replaced by divine life.

DECLARATION OF WHO YOU ARE:

The first step in working on your identity is openly declaring that you are a Christian. But unfortunately, some people already have trouble letting everyone know their identity in Christ. Some have refused to tell their friends or colleagues for fear of rejection. The first step to victory is your declaration that you are born again. If you desire to enjoy the benefits of salvation and be committed to Christ, you must be bold about your identity in Christ.

Hebrews 4:16 Let us therefore come boldly to the throne of grace that we may obtain mercy and find grace to help in time of need.

Matthew 11:12: And from the days of John the Baptist until now the kingdom of heaven suffers violence and the violent take it by force.

What causes a great ministry to emerge is the sound from heaven, your relationship with God. It is not your struggle. You are seeking the move and expression of God in time and building your monument in that move of God. The power of God is not in geographical location; it is in your relationship with Him. You must feel that God is within you, and His

Spirit lives in you. 1 John 4:4 You are of God, little children, and have overcome them because He who is in you is greater than he who is in the world.

When God gets ready to restore a church or a nation, He uses one man, and you can be that man. The devil is not after the masses, he is after one man, and he is after the giant killer God uses. Consider yourself blessed by God, not because of anything tangible; your blessing is beyond your cultural persuasion. God is faithful in challenging places.

Your declaration of who you are produces a new identity that fires you up to do the impossible in God's kingdom. When you declare who you are before men, the power of God is released through you into your world, creating the right atmosphere around you that will enhance your spiritual growth and that of others. It is a thing of honour and joy to be identified with Christ Jesus. Be assured that the problems, the fire, and the storms of life, floods, and desert places you go through know who you are when you declare and openly decree who you are.

It is the declaration of your identity that determines your productivity. You are not adopted in God's Kingdom to operate in the law of gravity, "everything that goes up must come down," But you are adopted in God's kingdom to be influenced by the law of aerodynamics. "Everything that goes up must stay up." You are regenerated to reign above conditions.

Luke 9:26-27 For whosoever is ashamed of Me, and My words, of him, the son of man will be ashamed when He comes in His own glory and in His Father's and of the holy angels but I tell you truly, there are some standing here who shall not taste death till they see the kingdom of God.

Job 13:15 though He slays me. Yet will I trust Him, even so, I will defend my own ways before Him.

You are not protected when you realize your life is a mess and that the enemy took advantage of you because of how you live and that you have not kept the walls up. With God, you can begin to build the right kind of life protection you need. If you feel the storms of life have overtaken you, continue to discover who you are and what you are created for through God's word; when you transform, you get the power to effect changes. God wants to magnify His name through you when you have a personal encounter with Him.

2 Corinthians 2:4 Now thanks be to God who always leads us in triumph in Christ and through us diffuses the fragrance of His knowledge in every place. For we are to God the fragrance of Christ among those who are being saved and among those who are perishing.

Your identity must smell Christ. Your identity must have the aroma of Christ within it.

When you encounter trials in life, they must smell Christ in you: When you go through pains, avalanches of storms and hurricanes of trials, mountains, valleys, floods, and desert places, they must all smell the Christ in you. The fragrance of Christ, which you are, destroys every demographic onslaught of the enemy. Faith inspires us to pray, but faith will command us to command. Prayer is without accomplishment unless it is accompanied by faith.

CHAPTER 21

PERSONIFIED INDIVIDUAL

When you have revelation, it makes you a voice. If you don't have your own revelation, you are only an echo because revelation is a revelation only when it is your own. The scope of your possession is defined by your own revelation. No revelation of your own means you echo someone else's revelation. What has God said about you?

Who are you is one question separating you from the natural and supernatural, health, depression, loneliness, poverty, plenty, lack, etc.? Many are who they are because people around them say so. If your crowd approves of you today, you have a good day; if they don't, you have a sad, ugly day. Many folks have lost who they are because they live on crowd approval. A compliment is genuine when it comes from self. Your crowd is not supposed to determine how you feel or your day. What should determine your day is the potential God has placed and deposited in your inner man.

Many look at you, but few see who you are. There are a lot of people looking at you, but they do not see you. Some people define you based on what they have been told and heard about you, irrespective of not being at the scene. These people don't know who you are until God reveals who you are. Man looks at the outward manifestations, but God looks at the inward man, the heart. The Lord does not see as man sees. (1 Samuel 16:7)

2 Corinthians 13:5 (NKJV) Examine yourself as to whether you are in the faith, test yourselves.

Do you not know yourselves that Jesus Christ is in you? -Unless you are disqualified vs6, But I trust that you will know that we are not disqualified.

You cannot claim to be a born-again Christian when you have a complex about yourself, God, or what people say about your image. You don't need to worry about compliments because if nobody compliments you, God has already done that; bless somebody because you are wonderfully made. With every hurt comes a lesson, and with every lesson, you get better.

God wants to bring your attitude into your altitude, and you must be confident in who God says you are. Because you are a star, a regenerated spirit, what you speak, what you hear, what you comprehend, and how you think must change. *Genesis*

1:28 says Fill the earth and subdue it and have dominion over the fish of the sea and over the birds of the air and over every living thing that moves on the earth.

1 John 4:4 You are of God, little children and have overcome them because greater is He that is in you than he that is in the world.

The God in you must come out and reign over your circumstances. When you worship materiality, you become material, and when you worship God, you become a spirit. Whatever you worship is what you become. If you serve God, you must manifest His potential. Do not worship the creation; instead, worship the Creator. When you hang around God, you will come out with a testimony. *Colossians 1:27 To them God willed to make known what are the riches of the glory of this mystery among the Gentiles; which is Christ in you, the hope of glory.*

Who are you? Some people confess with their head (their own reasoning) instead of voicing and visioning what God has deposited or destined them for. You don't need the glory of your crowd to be who God has called you to be. You don't need approval and compliments to realize you are good enough. Walk in the light of the potential God has deposited in you. Experience God personally as an individual, and you will find out who you are. *Amos 3:7 surely the Lord does nothing unless He reveals His secret to His servants, the prophets.*

ABRAHAMS' SEED:

Galatians 3:26-29 For you are all sons of God through faith in Christ Jesus. For as many of you as were baptized into Christ have put on Christ. There is neither Jew nor Greek, there is neither slave nor free, there is neither male nor female; for you are all one in Christ. And if you are Christ, then you are Abraham's seed and heirs according to the promise.

Your citizenship changed instantly when you were born again. Sometimes you hear people say, "I am from an average family," "I am from a poor family," and so on. Sadly, some Christians are among those that say such things. They say so because their focus is on their earthly lineage. And you become what your focus is. They focus on their earthly parents, grandparents, and other progenitors in reaching such a conclusion. You should realize there is another and more real family tree than you are looking at here on earth.

Ephesians 3:14-15 For this cause I bow my knees unto the Father of our Lord Jesus Christ of whom the whole family in heaven and earth is named.

Although you have an earthly parent, you are of the family of God because of your recreated spirit. Your focus should center on the promises of God and the legacy of God, not on the legacy of your earthly parents, some of whom carry curses because of their unregenerate spirits. You become instantly a carrier of blessings, purposes, and promises when you get born again. The curses of your parents and grandparents are no longer your portion.

Numbers 23:8 &23 sheds more light.

How shall I curse whom God has not cursed? And how shall I denounce whom the Lord has not denounced? Vs23 "For there is no sorcery against Jacob, nor any divination against Israel, It now must be said of Jacob and of Israel, Oh, what God has done.

2 Corinthians 5:17-18 Therefore, if anyone is in Christ, he is a new creation, old things have passed away; behold all things have become news. Now all things are of God, who has reconciled us to Himself through Jesus Christ and has given us the ministry of reconciliation.

When you are born again, you stop carrying generation curses; the curses of your parents and grandparents are no longer your portion because Jesus has nailed them on the cross in your stead. You become a child of the promise.

Genesis 22:17-18 That in the blessing, I will bless thee and in multiplying I will multiply thy seeds as the stars of the heaven and as the sand which is upon the sea shore and your seed shall possess the gate of his enemies. And in your seed shall all the nations of the earth be blessed because you have obeyed My voice.

God created the universe and gave Abraham great portions;

you, as Abraham's seed, have access to the blessings of Abraham because you are Abraham's seed. Galatians 3:29 And if you are in Christ, then you are Abraham's seed and heirs according to the promise.

Romans 11:29 (Living Bible) For God's gift and His call can never be withdrawn, He will never go back on His promises.

God does not change His mind about the volume of what is written. He does not change His mind on whom He chooses and blesses. This means Abraham's blessings are still working for our good even today. So, you are a beneficiary because you are in Christ, and hence you are Abraham's seed.

You have a new family tree because you are born again Christian. This family tree is not an average family that can be limited. You are born into an unlimited family tree.

Hebrews 12:22-24 But you have come to Mount Zion and to the city of the living God, the heavenly Jerusalem, to an innumerable company of angels to the general assembly and church of the first born who are registered in heaven, to God the judge of all, to the spirits of the just men made perfect. To Jesus the Mediator of the new covenant and to the blood of sprinkling that speaks better things than that of Abel.

Zion is the beautiful country where you belong to God's beloved people. There is no failure, recession or poverty, and sickness in Zion. No wonder the Bible says in Isaiah 33:24, *"Those that dwell therein shall not say, 'I am sick'* because *their sins have been forgiven."*

What an awesome God we serve. You have a divine origin; you are a citizen of Zion. Therefore, you are not subject to the principles of this world's system.

John 17:14-18 I have given them your word and the world has hated them because they are not of the world. I don't pray that you should take them out of the world but that you should keep them from evil one. They are not of the world; just as I am not of the world, sanctify them by Your truth, your word is the truth. As you sent Me into the world, I also have sent them into the world.

This means that although you have earthly parents and habitat because you are a Zion citizen, your earthly orientation does not determine your destiny and course of life. Though you respect your parents as commanded by the scriptures, they have no rule over your spirit. You can never inherit failure, blood disease, curses, or poverty. Every one of your seeds will be successful.

Isaiah 54:17 No weapon formed against you shall prosper, And every tongue which rises against you in judgment, you shall condemn. This is the heritage of the servants of the Lord.

So, when you think about your family tree, think about Abraham, Isaac, Jacob, David, John, Jesus, Paul, Peter, Stephen, Andrew, and all God's great men and women. Your family tree is a lineage of champions and winners. You have the greatest, wealthiest, and most sublime family identity, and it's the family of God. Walk in the great light of this truth always; be conscious of your identity and where you come from. If you are Abraham's seed, the blessings of God bestowed on Abraham will follow you automatically; you don't struggle for it.

You will not be dictating to God what He will do for you. Not many Christians have sat down to ask, *"What are those things God wants them to do for Him?"* Only mature Christians think and talk this way. It is usual for a young child to request for their parent to buy things each time they go out, but when they come to maturity, things change; instead, they ask their parents what they want or what household chores they want them to do.

In the same way, if you are born again, you can say, *"I asked the Lord to do something for me, and He did it"* But as you mature in the things of the Spirit, you begin to know what your household chores are in the kingdom of God, you humble yourself, and listen to God's instructions. The God we serve is a Sovereign God who reigns in awesome majesty.

Hebrews 12:2 Looking unto Jesus the author and Finisher of our faith, who for the joy that was set before Him endured the cross, despising the shame and is set down at the right hand of the throne of God.

Moses saw His presence; he said, *"I exceedingly fear and*

tremble" God does not exist for you; you live and exist for Him.

Revelation 4:11 Thou art worthy, O Lord, to receive glory and honor and power, for thou hast created all things and for Thy pleasure, they are and were created.

There must be a time in your life when you realize that Jesus is Lord of your life and that you belong to Him and exist for Him. Many Christians do not understand this yet; that's why they always make long request lists of what they want God to do for them. Your purpose on earth is to carry out His divine will; only then will you enjoy true fulfillment in life.

Isaiah 43:6-7 I will say to the north, give up and to the south, keep not back, bring My sons from far and my daughters from the ends of the earth even every one that is called by my name, for I have created him for my glory. I have formed him, yea, I have made him.

God is interested in the growth and development of your human spirit, for He knows that when your soul and spirit prosper, you will also prosper in your health, finances, and other areas of your life. It is essential that your spirit grows to maturity, for that's the only way you are guaranteed to live a successful life. Successful life is beyond buying a new car, owning a house or an estate, giving birth to a child, passing your exams, or landing a good job or contract. True success is living in God's perfect will and plan. And only those who have grown spiritually through the Word can discern God's perfect will.

Learn to invest your time in studying the Word of God, in prayers, soul-winning, and evangelism, and in spiritual activities like attending church services, prayer meetings, and spending quality time in fellowship with the Holy Spirit every day. Invest your resources and money in the kingdom of God by constantly sowing seeds into the furtherance of the gospel. Before long, there will be a bountiful harvest; you will experience tremendous growth in every area of your life. Invest your time and resources in things that matter, for time is short, and the Lord desires to do quick work in your life.

Genesis 8:22 While the earth remains, seedtime and harvest and cold and heat and summer and winter and day and night shall not cease.

Always remember and walk your family tree and know you are not an accident or failure on earth. You are created for a divine purpose.

Ephesians 2:12-14 & 18-21 That at that time you were without Christ, being aliens from the commonwealth of Israel and strangers from the covenants of promise, having no hope and without God in the world. But now in Christ Jesus you who once were far off have been brought near by the blood of Christ. For He Himself is our peace, who has made both one and has broken down the middle wall of separation between us. For through Him we both have access by one Spirit to the father. Now therefore you are no longer strangers and foreigners but fellow citizens with the saints and members of the household of God. Having been built on the foundation of the apostles and prophets, Jesus Christ Himself being the Chief Corner Stone. In whom the whole building been fitted together, grows into a holy temple in the Lord. In whom you also are built together for a dwelling place of God in the Spirit.

CHAPTER 22

THE CHARACTER OF YOUR THOUGHTS

Isaiah 33:20 & 24 Look upon Zion, the city of our solemnities, your eyes shall see Jerusalem a quiet habitation, a tabernacle that shall not be taken down, not one of the stakes thereof shall ever be removed neither shall any of the cords thereof be broken vs24 and the inhabitants shall not say "I am sick, the people that dwell therein shall be forgiven their iniquity.

The city prophet Isaiah is referring to is Zion, the city of the living God, and you were born into Zion at the point of conception when you received Christ as your Lord and Saviour.

Hebrews 12:22-23 But you have come to Mount Zion and to the city of the living God, the heavenly Jerusalem and to an innumerable company of angels to the general assembly and church of the first born which are written in heaven and to God the Judge of all and to the spirits of just men made perfect.

The citizens of Zion should not say they are sick because they are avoiding wrong confessions; instead, it is because their nature is void of sickness. They should not get sick. They are the possessors of eternal life, and that life destroys sickness, repels diseases, and annuls infirmities.

Some people speak words that change a situation, and others use words that change destiny. Those who change destiny are nation shakers. The pinnacle of your truth is that which leads you to a place of sovereignty, a place where any situation or circumstances cannot move you. You have a fixed position in this stead because of the authority and integrity of the Word of God. If you conceive the invisible, you can do the impossible. God uses submitted life to accomplish the impossible.

3 John 2 (NKJV) Beloved, I pray that you may prosper in all things and be in health, just as your soul prospers.

This way of life is rhetorical to some folks because they feel no one can be perpetually healthy. But this is the life Jesus brought to us. Beloved, notice that he didn't say, I wish above all things that you may prosper and be healed; instead, He said that you might prosper and be in health. He is talking about you living in divine health and not merely getting healed. Healing is a good thing, but it is the children's bread. It is lesser light; walking in divine health is a greater light. You must understand the truth when you are living in divine health; you don't need healing because you don't get sick.

1 Peter 2:24 Who Himself bore our sins in His own body on the tree that we having died to sins might live for righteousness- by whose stripes you were healed.

Someone says, but what if I feel sick? Will I not express how I feel? No, remember that your confession rules you. So, speak the word. You need to know that the presence of a symptom is not proof of sickness. The symptom shouldn't change your confession that divine health is yours in the now. Therefore, eradicate the sickness talk from your vocabulary and language completely. If you maintain your faith- confession that divine health is your present hour- possession, your body will be immune or protected from all sickness, infirmity, and diseases.

We have been called to live sickness-free and disease-free life. As you grow in Christ, you must leave the good things for the best. You need to transcend the level of needing healing from God to live every day in divine health. This is your birthright as a child of God.

When Satan deceived Adam and Eve in the Garden of Eden, he stole the Adamic authority from Adam, and when Adam disobeyed God, he acted on Satan's rebellious dictates. Now Adamic authority was higher than the angelic authority. But Jesus died and resurrected, giving us a higher authority than what Adam had, or Satan took from Adam. The Bible said that when Jesus died, we died with Him; when He was buried, we were buried with Him, and when He was raised, we were raised with Him. *(Ephesians 2:5-6) He is our authority.* We exercise dominion in the mighty name of Jesus Christ.

Luke 10:18-19 And He said unto them, I beheld Satan as lightening fall from heaven vs19 Behold, I give unto you power to tread on serpents and scorpions and over all the power of the enemy and nothing shall by any means hurt you.

The day you were born again, you were born into a life of total and continuous victory. Jesus' death on the cross made you one with Him and ushered you into the transcendent life of victory. Some folks believe life is full of "ups and downs," but that is because they are not acquainted with the vital realities and vitamins of the gospel of Christ. A believer's consciousness should be to live each day in victory over every situation; this should be a lifestyle.

2 Corinthians 2:14 Now thanks be to God, who always leads us in triumph in Christ and through us diffuses the fragrance of His knowledge in every place.

No challenge is big enough, and no demon is powerful enough to stop you from walking in victory. You only need to walk in the light of your victory. This means to live with the consciousness of a victor in Christ Jesus. It means to have a winning mentality, the mindset of a victor. *Romans 8:28 and we know that all things work together for good to those who love God, to those who are called according to His purpose.*

Matthew 16:19 And I will give unto thee, the keys of the kingdom of heaven and whatsoever thou shall bind on earth shall be bound in heaven and whatsoever thou shalt loose on earth shall be loosed in heaven.

Understand that when God looks at you, He does not see one who needs deliverance or help but one who should be acting in dominion. He sees you strong, full of the Holy Spirit and power. He sees one who is more than a conqueror. God does not want you to be eaten up by your emotions when ugly onslaughts are confronting you. He wants you to stay in dominion. You must agree with this picture of yourself.

You are the character of your thoughts, so when your thoughts are consistent with the provisions of God's Word, your life will reflect what God has said concerning you. The word of God is an agent of transformation.

And do not be conformed to this world but be transformed by the renewing of your mind that you may prove what is, that good and acceptable and perfect will of God (Romans 12:2).

Each time your inner man receives the word of God, God's thoughts are planted, and He starts to bombard your mind, thereby propelling His opinions and ideas to well up your inside. Your thoughts must be in sync with God's word if you will leave a victorious life. Thoughts have constructive and destructive potentials. *Proverbs 23:7 For as he thinks in his heart, so is he.*

When you realize your potential and identity, you become revolutionary to the onslaughts of life and become an instrument through which God's name is magnified.

Philippians 4:8 Finally brethren, whatsoever things are true, whatsoever things are honest, whatsoever things are just, whatsoever things are lovely, whatsoever things are of good report, if there be any virtue and if there be any praise, think on these things.

Philemon 1:6 states that the sharing of your faith may become effective by acknowledgment of every good thing which is in you in Christ Jesus.

MADE A KING WITH ACCESS TO ACT LIKE ONE:

Revelation 1:5-6 And from Jesus Christ, the faithful witness, the firstborn from the dead and the ruler over the kings of the earth. To Him who loved us and washed us from our sins in His own blood and has made us kings and priests to His God and Father, to Him be glory and dominion forever and ever. Amen.

A king does not beg, he issues a command, and it is carried out. This is the stand of a recreated spirit. You are created not to beg for things to happen but to issue commands in the full volume of what is written. *Job 22:28-29 You will declare a thing, And it will be established for you so light will shine on your ways.* When they cast you down, and you say, exaltation will come. Your influence over every situation that confronts you should be the influence of a king. Circumstance and situations should not rule you, but you rule over situations and circumstances. Exercising dominion in every onslaught and demographic limitations as a king is what you are made for. The light in you will not shine if you are extinguished.

Ecclesiastes 8:4 says, "Where the word of a king is, there is power and who may say to him "what are you doing?

When you take a stance as a king, you recognize your identity, and situations and storms of life will not question your capacity. They already know who you are, and as you issue your commands, they bow; situations bow at your command. God has supersaturated you with power and authority; you must know that power and authority do not sleep; they are to be demonstrated. *1 Corinthians 4:20-21 For the kingdom of God is not in word but in power. What do you want? Shall I come to you with a rod or in love and a spirit of gentleness?)*

Matthew 18:18 (NKJV) "Assuredly, I say to you, whatever you bind on earth will be bound in heaven and whatever you loose on earth will be loosed in heaven."

You are designed to effect changes; you rule in dominion as

a king to utter every demographic onslaught and hindrance of the enemy.

You are not created to reason like those in the world; your language should be positive. You don't tolerate or meditate on thoughts of fear, failure, and defeat. The consciousness of your righteousness will cause you to walk in dominion and speak with authority. When you listen to the prayer content of some believers, you will discover that it is full of inconsistencies with their kingly office. They say things like, "O God, I am begging you to please help me out of this trouble" That's the prayer language of the righteous.

Never beg God to do anything for you; pray in accordance with His Word and pray the promise and not the problem in the name of Jesus. This is how to pray as a righteous king-priest unto God. You are called to reign in life as a king, exercising dominion over the forces of nature and authority over circumstances inconsistent with God's will and word. Your words are backed with the power to alter negative situations into positive ones. Every word you speak today comes to pass in the name of Jesus Christ because you recognize your place as a righteous king-priest unto God.

Jeremiah 5:14 (NIV) Therefore, this is what the Lord God Almighty says "because the people have spoken these words, I will make my words in your mouth fire and these people wood and it consumes.

God is bigger than your doubts; if you stay hanging on to God, there is always a push on the inside to move you to higher frequencies. You can do the right thing for so long and miss the will of God for your life because of ignorance. Learn to trust in the ability of God; only a heart nourished in the word of God can stand in the hard places and dry grounds. Forget about "I can't"; it is not found in divine vocabulary, don't trust other people's faith, and have yours in God.

Ecclesiastes 7:7 (KJV) surely oppression makes a wise man mad and a gift destroys the heart vs12 for wisdom is a defense and money is a defense but the Excellency of knowledge is that wisdom gives life to them that have it.

You are not a failure. That your event failed does not mean that you are a failure. Your event failed for you to gain experience to try again. Delay does not mean denial. That your event was delayed does not mean you have been denied.

Ephesians 2:5-7 Even when we were dead in trespasses, He made us alive together with Christ by grace, you have been saved vs6 and raised us up together and made us sit together in heavenly places in Christ Jesus vs7 that in the ages to come He might show the exceeding riches of His grace in His kindness toward us in Christ Jesus.

CHAPTER 23

MANIFESTING THE ABILITY OF GOD WITHIN YOU

The most exciting thing I have ever learned about Redemption is God's marvellous and tremendous ability that is in a believer a recreated spirit.

"Wherefore if any man is in Christ, he is a new creation: the old things are passed away; behold, they are become new" (2 Corinthians 5:17).

What calls for notice here is that the believer is a New Creation. He is created in Christ Jesus. He is the workmanship of God. This New Creation has become a reality to him because he has received the life and nature of God.

1 John 5:13 "These things I have written to you, that you may know that you have eternal life, even to you that believe on the name of the Son of God.

You have within you the life and nature of God as a believer. 2 Peter 1:4 tells us that we have become partakers of the divine nature,

"Whereby He has granted unto us His precious and exceeding great promises; that through these you may become partakers of the divine nature, having escaped from the corruption that is in the world by lust."

Jesus emphasizes this by His illustration, *"I am the vine, you are the branches" (John15:5).* The object of His coming was that we might have life and have it abundantly.

John 10:10b" I came that they may have life, and may have it abundantly."

You received Eternal life. That Eternal life is the nature of the Father as unveiled in Christ. As a branch of the Vine is flowing out through you and bearing fruit. It is the vine's life in you that produces fruitage of love, faith, and joy. It is not the Vine that bears fruits but the branches, so you are individually the fruit-bearer, not God.

YOU HAVE GOD'S WORD ABIDING IN YOU

Some people speak words that change a situation; others speak words that change destiny. Those who change destinies are nation shakers and destiny makers.

Colossians 3:16 "Let the word of Christ dwell in you richly."

What is it doing there? It is admonishing, nourishing, it is educating, it is training, it is correcting, and it is building faith and love into your spirit.

Acts 20:32" Now I commend you to God and to the word of His grace, which is able to build you up and to give you the inheritance among all them that are sanctified."

It is the word that builds up. It is the word that informs you about your inheritance. It is the word that unveils your relationship and fellowship to the Father-God. It is the word that declares your rights and privileges in Christ. It is the words of Jesus Christ that healed most of the people who came to Him. He said they were His Father's words.

The Pauline Revelation is the Father's words about Jesus.

When you are a New Creation in Christ, The Father's words must supersaturate you and express fact through your lips. When you say, **"In the Name of Jesus,"** diseases stop being, you are using the Father's words that He spoke through Jesus' lips.

When you hang on and step out into your rights of righteousness and begin to express them to bear fruit, it will be the same kind of fruit Jesus bore in His earthly walk. Righteousness means the ability to stand in the Father's presence without a sense of guilt or inferiority.

This Righteousness became yours through the finished work of Christ. *Romans 4:25 "Who was delivered up for our trespasses and was raised for our justification" A literal translation of this verse reads: "Who was delivered up on account of our trespasses and raised when we were declared Righteous."*

When the life of God is liberated, the ability of God as unveiled in the word is let loose. They tell us there is power enough in an atom to propel a great ship across the ocean. If the power that is invested in the life of God that is in you and the power that is invested in the word of God (that word that spoke a universe into being) were let loose in you, things would happen, wouldn't they? The focus of this write-up is that God wants to be set free in you. The words we speak are spiritual containers that hold either faith or fear. You can create the life you want and live it in abundance or abject poverty. Words are the tools of communication, and words have multiple meanings, and the context of speech you make reveals which meaning is preferred.

Isaiah 50:4 "The Lord God has given me the tongue of the learned, that I should know how to speak a word in season to him who is weary. He awakens me morning by morning. He awakens my ear, to hear as the learned."

Christianity is not decoration; not everybody is fit for mental deliberation, especially in God's kingdom. Think carefully and take counsel. Mutual interaction of hope and faith will give you dominion over everything you dream of having. Every progress has a price tag on it. Becoming someone who never gives up will cost you something; it will need sacrifice. You will never get where you want to be in life without being willing to sacrifice and push through obstacles and adversities that stand in your way.

Find the areas where you are not experiencing success and reflect on what God thinks about your ability to progress and the volume of what is written- the word of God concerning those areas. If you are stagnate, you will find that your mindset is the cause and reason why you are. You cannot make a success if your mind is beclouded with negative thoughts. A prosperous life starts with a prosperous mind.

God cannot glorify Himself in your life without consciousness on your part of who you are as a person and what God's word says about you. The word of God imbibes God's illumination; if a man is sloppy with diet, his physical body suffers; if a man is sloppy with the word of God, his spirit suffers. If you want muscles, you must train in fitness, which applies to your spiritual muscles.

YOU HAVE THE NAME OF JESUS AS YOUR INSTRUMENT:

The Name of Jesus echoes with great thunderous authority. The name Jesus Christ produces results when mentioned.

Anyone who calls that Name with the understanding of the power vested therein will undoubtedly have the right results. A name is more than a mere article of identification. A name depicts "authority" or "character." The ability to act is in the Name of Jesus Christ. There is a delegated authority that affects changes in using that wonderful Name. It can unmake ugly situations. It can give you beauty for ashes, the oil of joy for mourning, and the garment of praise for the Spirit of the Lord.

John 14:13-14 "Whatever you shall ask (or demand) in my name, that will I do, that the Father may be glorified in the Son. If you shall ask anything in My Name, that will I do.

This is not praying to the Father nor making a request of Jesus. It is using the Name as Peter used it at the Beautiful Gate when he set that man free from infantile paralysis.

The Greek word is "ONOMAH," so when you command something to happen in the name of Jesus Christ, you are speaking or acting in the authority or character of Jesus Christ. This is the power of attorney Christ has given to you. When you make a demand in the name of Jesus Christ, you don't need to squeeze up faith to make it work. The Name Jesus is faith in evidence; that's because faith is evidence, the evidence of unseen realities, and when unseen realities become available, you no longer need any unseen reality. It is an instrument that has already been made available to you. *The Bible says in Acts 4:12, "There is none other name under heaven given among men, whereby we must be saved."*

The Name Jesus Christ has been given to you as a gift without cross-examination, so you need no extra faith to use the Name.

Isaiah 43:7 & 11 Even every one that is called by My Name; for I have created him for my glory. I have formed him; yea I have made him, I even I, am the Lord and beside Me, there is no Saviour.

Colossians 3:17 And whatever you do in word or deed, do all in the Name of the Lord Jesus, giving thanks to God the father through Him.

Philippians 2:9-11 Therefore God also has highly exalted Him and given Him the Name which is above every name that at the Name of Jesus every knee should bow, of those in heaven and of those on earth and of those under the earth and that every tongue should confess that Jesus Christ is Lord, to the glory of God the Father.

It commands the forces of darkness to become obedient to the authority of the Name of Jesus. That Name is yours. You may not have taken advantage of it. Jesus gave you the power of attorney to use His Name. He said in Matthew 28:18-19, *"All authority has been given to Me in heaven and on earth. Go you therefore and make "disciples"* means student, one who learns. We are to make students of the Word of all nations. You have the ability to go and do it. *"In my name they shall cast out demons—they shall lay hands on the sick, and they shall recover (Mark 16:17-18)*. This belongs to you. The age of miracle is your age; it is this present age. You can live and walk in the fullness of God's ability. You can let that ability be transmitted through you if you will. This is love's challenge to allow the life of God to be transmitted through you, to let the Word spread through you, to give the name its real place in your life.

A TRANSMITTER OF LOVE

Romans 8:19 (NIV) For the creation waits in eager expectation for the children of God to be revealed.

Your identification with Him puts you on the throne. His identification with you puts you in the place of leaders, teachers, comforters, helpers, and burden-bearers. You bring God to man, just as He came to us. You are love as He is love. You are His love lips and feet. Without wires, the mighty generator of Coulee Dam would be helpless; without transmitters, God in all His ability is helpless. His love can find no expression except through New Creation. Those great generators are dependent on wires. They alone can bear the current that can stir the motors and light the world's homes. If you fail God, He is helpless. You limit Him, or we allow Him to be limitless. The church has been weak and powerless. Sin has reigned as a master, and the church has served as a slave. Yet the church represents the New Creation which is a Satan-conqueror. When the truth gains ascendancy in us, it will make us spiritual supermen, masters of demons and diseases.

Matthew 5:13-16 You are the salt of the earth but if the salt loses its flavor, how shall it be seasoned? It is then good for nothing but to be thrown out and trampled underfoot by men. You are the light of the world, a city that is set on hill cannot be hidden nor do they light a lamp and put it under a basket but on a lamp stand and it gives light to all who are in the house. Let your light shine before men that they may see your good works and glorify your father in heaven.

FAITH AN ACCESS

Isaiah 32:17 The work of righteousness shall be peace and the effect of righteousness, quietness and confidence forever.

The work of righteousness that God did in your life has brought peace to your heart.

Romans 8:1- 2 There is therefore now no condemnation to them that are in Christ Jesus".

You live in perfect quietness and rest. The effect of righteousness on your heart is a new quietness and a new type of faith. You enjoy the effect of your confidence in the finished work of

Christ on the cross.

Romans 10:17 So then faith comes by hearing and hearing by the word of God. What you hear is where your faith is, you can only have faith in what you hear, because what you hear becomes your mindset. Galatians 3:26 For we are all sons of God through faith in Christ Jesus.

You know that you have become the master of circumstances. You are master over demons. You are effective, you lay hands on the sick, and they are healed.

Realizing this truth gives you a sense of quietness and a fullness of joy you have never enjoyed. The phrase "confidence forever" is striking. You have moved out of the restless atmosphere of fear and doubt into the realm of quiet waters of victory.

You have become a master where you once served as a slave. You are a conqueror where you suffered defeat. You walk in the light where you walked in darkness. You enjoy your privileges in Christ. You have your own faith, and you have arrived.

John 15:5 "I am the Vine; ye are the branches: He that abides in Me, and I in him, the same bears much fruit: for apart from Me ye can do nothing."

You enjoy the consciousness of the life of the Vine abiding in you. You are the fruit-bearing part of Christ. You have been grafted into Him by the New Birth. This graft has given you a new nature that makes you bear the Jesus kind of fruit, which is love and faith fruits.

His word on your lips produces real results. His word on your lip is God-talking. The Father's Word in Jesus' lips healed the sick. His Word on your lips is the same because you know you abide in Him. You bear the fruitage of His indwelling Word.

You have legal rights, and whatever you demand is commanded, and He gives to you. Whatever your tongue says is established, whatever you speak, you've taken, whatever you bind is bound, and whatever you loose is loosed. Your tongue is a ready writer.

Psalm 45:1 My heart is overflowing with a good theme; I recite my composition concerning the king; my tongue is the pen of a ready writer.

John 16:23-24 Jesus said, "In that day you shall ask me nothing: Verily verily, I say unto you, if you shall ask anything of the father, He will give it to you in my name."

The word ask here means "Demand," It is used not in the sense that you command him to give, but in the sense that you go into the bank and demand payment on your check. In the same sense, your faith takes rights, its portion.

James 1:22-24 "But be doers of the word and not hearers only, deceiving yourselves. For if anyone is a hearer of the word and not a doer, he is like a man observing his natural face in a mirror; for he observes himself and goes away and immediately forgets what kind of man he was".

You have become a doer of the word, not just a hearer; you do not delude or deceive yourself with false hopes. You are in Christ, an heir of God and a joint heir with Jesus Christ. You are aware that his word abides in you and produces results. You are a producer. You are not making time longer. You know what kind of man you are, a New Creation, empowered by God. Faith is substance, a mightiness of reality, a deposit of divine nature, the creative God within. Faith takes you to the place where God reigns. As you die to the human desire, there comes a fellowship within perfected cooperation, you are ceasing and God increasing in you. God in you is a living substance, a spiritual nature. *Romans 1:17 For in it the righteousness of God is revealed from faith to faith; as it is written, "The just shall live by faith."*

Hebrews 11:1-3 & 6 Now faith is the substance of things hoped for, the evidence of things not seen vs2 For by it the elders obtained a good testimony vs3 By faith we understand that the worlds were framed by the word of God, so that the things which are seen were not made of things which are visible. Vs6 But without faith it is impossible to please Him for he who comes to God must believe that He is and that He is a rewarder of those who diligently seek Him.

If you refused to act your faith, you have no testimony; if

there is no testimony, the promise has been made of no effect. *Romans 4:14 For if those who are of the law are heirs, faith is made void and the promise made of no effect.*

Because of God's love, you should know that hope does not disappoint us; your hope has evidence, and the evidence of hope is faith.

Romans 5:5-6 Now hope does not disappoint because the love of God has been poured out in our hearts by the Holy Spirit who was given to us vs6 For when we were still without strength, in due time Christ died for the ungodly.

KNOWLEDGE OF DISCERNMENT:

Discernment is the ability to distinguish between the Spirit of truth and the spirit of error, to spot subtle forms of phoniness and deception. *1 Corinthians 12:10 To another the working of miracles, to another prophecy, to another discerning of spirits, to another different kinds of tongues, to another the interpretation of tongues.* An example: Peter and Ananias and Sapphira in Acts Chapter 5.

Knowledge of discernment has to do with keen and deep insight, with a demonstration of sound judgment. This is a special type of knowledge with participation. You are involved with that knowledge as a New Creation. There is a relationship between you and that which you know.

Living in a positive frame of mind is being determined and being determined is having a positive mind of your life through your thoughts. You must learn to have thoughts of hope, prosperity, and visioning yourself as an overcomer even amid the storms of life. Encourage yourself every day to choose what kind of attitude you should have. You cannot be successful when your thoughts are messed up.

Go out every day expecting good things to happen to you. Your life is like a car that responds to different directions depending on which gear you accelerate. Set your mind always for victory. You can recondition your mind for success. Get up every day expectant that it is a great day.

You can give spirit to your physical body by starting to see the best in every situation. Expect your plans to succeed and have the mindset that if anything good will happen to anybody today, it will happen first to you. We have the mind of Christ (1 Corinthians 2:16). Learn to vision every obstacle as your opportunity to advance.

David did not give up on the appearance of the physical Goliath. His focus was on the greatness of the God he served. And because of David's discerning spirit, God made him see spiritually how small Goliath was in the realm of the spirit. For every great adversity, there is a great opportunity. You are created not to talk problems but to talk solutions. God at creation did not discuss darkness, but He spoke the solution, which is light into being. The credibility gap has been that

Christians are not imitating the footprints of Christ. When you are supersaturated with the Holy Ghost, He makes you discern what the truth is and what error is, for we have millions of information coming into the mind every second, and they all need to be filtered.

MADE ALIVE WITH CHRIST:

Colossians 2:13 "And you, being dead through your trespasses and the uncircumcision of your flesh, you I say, did he make alive together with Him."

Ephesians 2:5 "Even when we were dead through our trespasses, made us alive together with Christ.

This is the core and heart of Redemption. *Romans 6:5 "For if we have become united with Him in the likeness of His death, we shall be also in the likeness of His resurrection."*

Here we witness the miracle of Eternities. It took place in that subterranean prison house of death. Jesus was made alive.

Acts 13:33 "God hath fulfilled the same unto our children, in that he raised up Jesus; as also it is written in the second psalm, Thou art my Son, this day have I begotten thee."

Paul, by the Spirit, gave us *Colossians 1:18 "And He is the head of the body, the church: who is the beginning, THE FIRSTBORN FROM THE DEAD; that in all things He might have the preeminence."*

He was dead with our death. He had died twice spiritually and physically.

1 Peter 3:18 "Because Christ also suffered for sins once, the righteous for the unrighteous, that he might bring us to God; being put to death in the flesh but made alive in the spirit. This was not the Holy Spirit; this was rather His Spirit. What a transformation must have taken place. How it must have shaken the foundation of that awful place when they saw Him made alive, break the bonds of spiritual death and hurl back the forces of death that had overwhelmed Him on the cross. Now we can understand

Ephesians 2:10 "We are his workmanship, created in Christ" When were we created? In mind of justice, it was when Jesus was recreated down there. That is when the church was really born of God.

YOU ARE MADE RIGHTEOUS:

Righteousness means the ability to stand in the presence of the Father God without a sense of guilt or inferiority. God has dealt with the sin problem in His son. He has put sin away by the sacrifices of his Son. He has made it possible on legal grounds for a man who is spiritually dead, in union with Satan, to become a New Creation by receiving the very nature and life of God. Until a man is righteous and knows it, Satan reigns over him; sin and disease are his masters. But the instant he knows that he is the Righteousness of God in Christ and knows what that Righteousness means, Satan is defeated.

Man has a highly developed Sin Consciousness, a spirit inferiority complex, and a sense of unworthiness that dominates him. He is doubt ruled. All he has is Senses knowledge of faith that he cannot know God nor find him. Man is a spirit being, has a soul, and lives in a body. The real man can never be permanently satisfied with the things of the senses. Righteousness means that one could receive Eternal Life, which is the very nature of God.

Romans 5:1 Therefore, having been justified by faith, we have peace with God through our Lord Jesus Christ.

We are declared righteous through faith not by merit but because of Jesus's sacrifice on the cross for us. A man cannot be in Christ and have the devil's nature in him. He is either in the family of God or in the family of Satan. *1 John 3:10 "In this the children of God are manifest and the children of the devil."*

If you are living a life of weakness and defeat, you do not know what you are in Christ. Colossians 1:21-22 *"Being in time past alienated and enemies in your mind in your evil works, yet now has he reconciled in the body of His flesh through death, to present you holy and without blemish and unreprovable before Him. This has already been done in Christ and you stand before Him complete in Christ.*

You are made alive with Him in the mind of justice. This life is the nature of the Father, and when He received that nature, He became Righteous once more. He had been made sin. The moment that He was made alive, God justified Him.

He was made Righteous with the life of God as you are made Righteous in the New Creation. If He was made Righteous, then you who accept Him as your Savior, confess Him as your Lord, and receive Eternal life are automatically made Righteous that moment and can dominate the forces of hell in His Name.

Ephesians 4:24 and that you put on the new man which was created according to God, in true righteousness and holiness.

The same Eternal Life or nature of God that made Jesus Righteous has been imparted to us in the New Birth. Was it any wonder that the Spirit said through John, "As He is, so are we in this world."

2 Corinthians 5:21 "Him who knew no sin, he made to be sin on our behalf; that we might become the righteousness of God in Him."

Romans 3:26 "That he might Himself be righteous and the righteousness of him that hath faith in Jesus" (literal Trans).

You have become the righteousness of God in Christ; this righteousness is not an experience, although it gives birth to many marvelous experiences. It is the nature of the Father imparted to you. It is that nature gaining the ascendency in you until you know that you are what God says you are.

God became the Righteousness of Jesus, and the moment you accept Christ as Savior, confess Lord, and believe that God raised Him from the dead, He becomes your Righteousness. As God became the Righteousness of Jesus, He became the Righteousness of the New Creation.

Sin consciousness can be traced to the reason for practically every spiritual failure. It destroys faith; it destroys the initiative in the heart. It gives man an inferiority complex. He is afraid of God. He is afraid of himself. He is constantly searching to find someone that can pray the prayer of faith for him. He has no sense of responsibility and no sense of his legal right to stand in the Father's presence without condemnation.

God has made provision to make a New Creation; He has planned to impart His nature to him, taking out the old sin nature and replacing it with His nature. This will destroy sin consciousness. Sin consciousness is practically the parent of all human religions. Man has sought to heal this awful disease. The sense of unworthiness destroys faith, robs you of your peace of mind, and makes ineffectual the most earnest and zealous prayer life.

Ephesians 2:6 "And raised us up with Him and made us to sit with Him in the heavenly places, in Christ Jesus."

The sense of oneness with Him is as real as His sense of oneness was with you when He was made sin and sickness. You should arise and take a stand and your heritage as victors, as conquerors. Go out and do the work Jesus began to do when He was here.

The believer stands complete in Christ. He has partaken of the fullness of God in Christ.

John 1:16 "For of His fullness have we all received and grace upon grace.

Righteousness restores to man all that he lost in the fall, plus a new relationship as a son with all its privileges. The greatest freedom is not political freedom, freedom from financial worry or physical discomfort, but freedom from Sin Consciousness. Righteousness gives you the sweet consciousness of sonship privileges. The secret of victory is acting fearlessly, confessing boldly, because Satan fears you. You are the righteous man.

CRUCIFIED WITH CHRIST:

When Paul said, *"I have been crucified with Christ,"* it meant he had been judged, condemned, cast out, stripped naked, and nailed to the cross. The thought of crucifixion to a Jew and especially to a Pharisee brought a sense of shame and horror. When Saul of Tarsus identified himself with the man, Jesus, accepted Him as his savior and confessed His Lordship, that moment, he became a crucified man. Still, to the Jewish people, he became an outcast. No wonder he said in Galatians 6.14 that the world had been crucified unto him, and he had been crucified unto the world.

When you realize that you are crucified with Christ, you can no longer be deceived because you know the cruelty of being deceived. And you begin to know that there is nothing in you that the world desire. You see your identification with Christ in His crucifixion. Crucifixion does not mean death but union with Christ in His disgrace and suffering.

Romans 6:6 *Knowing this that our old man was crucified with him, that the body of sin might be done away, that so we should no longer be in bondage to sin.*

In the Spirit's great argument of our identification with Christ, he said that our old man, this hidden man of the heart, our spirit, the real man who was filled with spiritual death and satanic nature, was nailed to the cross in Christ. Christ was not there for Himself but as a substitute for us.

So, you were nailed to the cross with Christ. You were crucified with Him. The object of the crucifixion, in the mind of the mob, was to get rid of this man they hated. In the sense of justice, it meant His identification with humanity in its sin and suffering, and your identification with Him is His crucifixion.

FILLED INDWELLING HOLY SPIRIT:

The Holy Spirit is the greatest magnifier of life, the gifts, and the ministry of Jesus. And Jesus the King, when the Holy Ghost comes, is coroneted in the process of coronation, the Holy Ghost comes into the body, Jesus becomes King, and the Holy Ghost becomes the revealer of Kingship. A personal acquaintance with the Lord Jesus by the revelation of the Spirit can so move you that in an instant, you may have the revelation that would cause you to see that an enthronement or wisdom now encases you from on high.

2 Corinthians 2:12 Now we have received not the spirit of the world but the Spirit who is from God, that we might know the things that have been freely given to us by God.

Ignorance hinders and makes you suffer to struggle.

Ephesians 5:18-20 And do not be drunk with wine, in which is dissipation; but be filled with the Spirit vs19 speaking to one another in psalms and hymns and spiritual songs, singing and making melody in your heart to the Lord. vs20 giving thanks always for all things to God the Father in the Name of our Lord Jesus Christ.

There is a place where you can live in the anointing and the clothing of the Spirit, where your words will be clothed with power. It is a wonderful privilege to be clothed with the mantle of God. All reasoning and human knowledge cannot be compared with the power of life in the Spirit; we have the power to loose and bind.

Matthew 16:19 And I will give you the keys of the kingdom of heaven and whatever you bind on earth will be bound in heaven and whatever you loose on earth will be loosed in heaven.

There is a place where the Holy Ghost can put you where you cannot be anywhere else but in the presence of God and spirit. You cannot bind things in human strength or with the natural mind. The Prophet Ezekiel compelled himself to be in the Spirit before prophesying to the dry bones (Ezekiel 37). You cannot prophesy to your dry bones by being in human nature or exercising human strength.

Isaiah 11:1-3, there shall come forth a Rod from the stem of Jesse, and a Branch shall grow out of his roots vs2 The Spirit of the Lord shall rest upon him, The Spirit of wisdom and understanding, The Spirit of counsel and might. The Spirit of knowledge and of the fear of the Lord vs3 His delight is in the fear of the Lord, And He shall not judge by the sight of His eyes, nor decide by the hearing of His ears.

Jesus promised the disciples that the Holy Spirit, who was

with them, should be in them. On the day of Pentecost, he entered their bodies after He had recreated them. What a miracle it is to have God in us. It is tremendous to have His word dwell and abide in us when we already know that His word has created the universe, and we have that creative ability.

1 John 4:4 "You are of God, My little children and have overcome them: because greater is He that is in you than he that is in the world. The God in us is the same God who spoke a universe into being. The same God is in us who walked the sea in Galilee. The same God is in us who arose from the dead.

Philippians 2:13 "For it is God who is at work within you."

We have not taken advantage of the riches of grace that belongs to us; how few of us have let God loose in us. To the extent that it looks like God is struggling to have His place and to have His rights in the individual members of the body of Christ. How God longs to heal the sick, mend the broken-hearted, and break the power of Satan over the lives of men through us. Let us let Him loose in us.

When you are supersaturated with the conviction that Jesus is Lord of all, this conviction controls your attitude, how you talk, what you hear, and what you think makes you valuable to God. You can only be a witness when you experience the power of God.

The first Church in Jerusalem was formed by fire. Peter, the weakest apostle, became fire and bold and preached the gospel, and three thousand people were won for Christ. Divine order is far above our finite planning. Stephen was a man so filled with divine power. Although serving tables might have been alright in the minds of the other disciples, God had a more excellent vision for him- a baptism of fire, power, and divine anointing, that took him on and on to the climax of his life until he saw right into the open heavens.

As we go deeper into God, He enlarges our understanding and places before us a wide-open door, and I am not surprised that this man chosen to serve tables was afterward called to a higher plane. People know when the tide is flowing and when it is ebbing. Stephen began in a most humble place and ended in a blaze of glory. If there is anything in your life that resists the power of the Holy Spirit and the entrance of His word into your heart and life, drop on your knees and cry out loud for mercy. Your earnest campaign should be for God to envelop you with His Holy Ghost so that you can be a witness to the fireworks of God. *"But tarry ye in the city, until ye be clothed with ability from on high" (Luke 24:49)*

Acts 6:15 "And all who sat in the council, looking steadfastly at him, saw his face as the face of an angel."

Stephen's aim was high, and God brought his faithfulness with little to full fruition. Under the inspiration of divine power by which he spoke, his opponents could not help but listen. Even the angels listened, for he spoke with holy, prophetic utterance.

The ministry of the Holy Spirit is to make you fruitful, productive, and effective in every area of your life. He produces life in you because He is the life-giver. It makes no difference how deep in the valley a man may find himself in life; he needs to be more acquainted with the person of the Holy Spirit, and things will change.

WHAT COUNTS:

It is the value that will count in our Lord's final consideration of our earthly life and ministry. What is your value? What you have done with your life here on earth will show your value when Jesus Christ returns. Your value is not your cars, your houses, your estates, your children, your education, and your degrees but the impact on the Kingdom of God. Heaven has been counting for you from day one since you got recreated.

2 Corinthians 5:10 For we must all appear before the judgment seat of Christ that each one may receive the things done in the body (church) according to what he has done whether good or bad.

The credibility gap has been that salvation is by grace does not mean what you do does not really matter.

1 Corinthians 3:11-15 says, For no other foundation can anyone lay than that which is laid, which is Jesus Christ vs12 Now if anyone builds on this foundation with gold, silver, precious stones, wood, hay, straw vs13 each one's work will become clear; for the day will declare it, because it will be revealed by fire and the fire will test each one's work, of what sort it is vs14 If anyone's work which he has built on endures, he will receive a reward vs15 If anyone's work is burned, he will suffer loss but he himself will be saved, yet so as through the fire.

There are two kinds of materials to build in God's kingdom, those materials that burn and those that don't. Since every material is to be tried by fire, it is vital to build with fireproof materials. Everything that has no eternal value cannot survive the test of fire. So, if your identity has no eternal value, it will not survive the test of fire. Your identity and works must be redemptive to have any value before God because He is a redemptive God.

1 Peter 2: 1-6 Therefore, laying aside all malice, all deceit, hypocrisy, envy and all evil speaking vs2 as newborn babies, desire the pure milk of the word that you may grow thereby vs3 If indeed you have tested that the Lord is gracious vs4 coming to Him as to a living stone, rejected indeed by men but chosen by God and precious vs5 you also, as living stones are being built up a spiritual house, a holy priesthood, to offer up spiritual sacrifices acceptable to God through Jesus Christ vs6 Therefore it is also contained in the scripture Behold I lay in Zion, A chief cornerstone, elect precious and he who believes on Him will by no means be put to shame.

The precious or costly stones are living believers, built into a holy temple where God resides in His people. Our work and identity must be built on the proper foundation, Jesus Christ. God must be in it, it must be redemptive, and it must involve people being rightly related to God as his dwelling place. Our God will like to fully use His body, the church in which you are one in your identity. He will also enjoy the full habitation of His royal residence.

John 17: 15-16 I do not pray that You should take them out of the world but that You should keep them from the evil one. vs16 They are not of the world, just as I am not of the world.

You are living in the world, but you are a stranger here because you are not of this world. This consciousness should be digested by your spirit man. The worldly identity, so to speak, is not in your identity; you can have accolades, education, degrees, names, children, houses and cars, wives, and husbands, but these don't make up your identity. Your real identity is revealed in Christ. Therefore, our God is busy changing names before he uses you for His divine appointment. Simon Peter was called the Rock, Abram – Abraham, Jacob- Israel, Saul-Paul, etc. God changes your identity to align with His divine purpose and appointment.

YOU ARE CHOSEN BY GOD:

1 Peter 2:9-10 But you are a chosen race, a royal priesthood, a holy nation, a people for God's own possession, that you may proclaim the excellencies of Him who has called you out of darkness into His marvellous light for you once were not a people but now you are the people of God. You had not received mercy but now you have received mercy.

You were chosen to proclaim the excellencies of God, who called you out of darkness into marvelous light. You are not just ordinary. You are not a human being without a purpose. You are planted for a divine purpose to fulfil a mission; you are not a happenstance. Your identity is found in the divine purpose of God, which portrays who you are, and what gives you a divine identity is not colour, not your culture, your name, or your education. Still, you have a divine identity because God has chosen you. You are chosen though you did not merit it or earn it. It happened when you were born again, and your spirit was recreated at that point of conception. It is this identity that leads to your destiny. You are chosen, pitied, possessed, and declared holy by God to be a minister for God, a priest for God. When you identify yourself, you can identify your destiny.

Your identity is to proclaim the excellencies of the One who called you out of darkness into his marvellous light. God made you who you are so that you will proclaim the Excellencies of His freedom in choosing you, the Excellency of his grace in pitying you, and the Excellency of His authority and power in possessing you. God has given you identity so His identity might be proclaimed through you. God made you who you are so you can know who He is. Your identity is for the sake of making known His identity. Your identity means that the Excellency of God is seen in you.

John 1:4-5 & 9 In Him was life and the life was the light of men. Vs5 and the light shines in the darkness and the darkness did not comprehend it. Vs9 that was the true light which gives light to every man coming into the world.

Your identity cannot be an identity without a full fellowship with God. Your joy cannot be complete with an individual encounter and fellowship with Him. God is light: as long you fellowship with Him, you become a light to your world, and you walk in the light of the Father.

1 John 1:7 But if we walk in the light as He is in the light, we have fellowship with one another and the blood of Jesus cleanses us from all sin.

We have lived so long in the realm of the senses that it is difficult for us to realize what we are in Christ. There is no love and faith in the natural heart. But faith and love spring from a recreated spirit.

1 Corinthians 2:14 But the natural man does not receive the things of the Spirit of God: for they are foolishness to him: neither can he know them, because they are spiritually discerned.

THE NEW CREATION:

If you are born ageing, you are a new creation because your spirit has been recreated.

2 Corinthians 5:17 Therefore if anyone is in Christ, He is a new creation, old things have passed away, behold, all things have become new.

Jesus gave you the ability to use His words, His name that has all authority. Every demon knows that you are the recreated spirit given the power to operate in God's stead.

Luke 10:19 Behold, I give unto you power to tread on serpents and scorpions and over all the power of the enemy: and nothing shall by any means hurt you.

Mark 16:17 -18 And these signs shall follow them that believe, in my name shall they cast out devils; they shall speak with new tongues. They shall take up serpents; and if they drink any deadly thing, it shall not hurt them; they shall lay hands on the sick and they shall recover.

Matthew 28:18-19 And Jesus came and spoke to them saying, "All authority has been given to Me in heaven and on earth. Go therefore, and make disciples of all nations, baptizing them in the name of the Father and of the Son and of the

Holy Ghost, teaching them to observe all things that I have commanded you; and lo, I am with you always, even to the end of the age. Amen.

Psalm 82:6 I have said you are gods; all of you are the children of the Most High.

You are gods to every environment, god to demographic onslaughts of the enemy, gods to circumstances and situations. You become a god in every environment you enter, to sickness and diseases and every circumstance that is not to the glory of God Almighty.

The demon can only rule you by subterfuge, bluff, or deception. They put diseases upon you and hold you in bondage through ignorance of what you are in Christ and what belongs to you. Until man receives eternal life, the nature of God, he cannot exercise faith, and he cannot love. He will only have a sense of knowledge and faith. It is your decision, not your condition, that determines your future. Identity is for priestly service, proclaiming the Excellencies of God who called you. A believer is a possessor, "he that believes has eternal life."

Isaiah 61:6, but you shall be named the priest of the Lord. They shall call you the servants of our God. You shall eat the riches of the gentiles and in their glory you shall boast. Vs7 Instead of your shame, you shall have double honor. And instead of confusion, they shall rejoice in their portion. Therefore in their land they shall possess double, everlasting joy shall be theirs.

Demonstrate your identity; Apostle Paul did; that is why he was able to say boldly in *Philippians 4:13, "I can do all things through Christ who strengthens me."* Your identity is for demonstration of power to the glory of God.

1 Corinthians 4:20 for the kingdom of God is not in word, but in power.

YOU HAVE ABILITIES:

Make up your mind that you will have the alarm clock in your soul. You must have that spirit that conquers. "I vowed I would do it and have done it." There may be an untrained voice, untrained musical abilities, and other undiscovered abilities lying hidden under the careless, thoughtless exterior. Let us go down with a flashlight and look over the untouched treasures stored away inside that have never been touched or used. Let us bring the thing we find, make it worthwhile, and give it commercial value.

There is a gold mine hidden in every life. Nature never made a failure. Every man has success hidden away in his soul and no one else can find it himself; every individual holds the key to the hidden room. Failure emanates because we tried to find it somewhere else where it is not hidden. You can't do it anywhere else. Success, victory, and achievement are deposited in you. The exceptional and extraordinary people are those who develop what is within them. Geniuses have grown up to weeds just because they did not develop what they had.

The harnessed ability in you is worthwhile, an ability under intelligent mastery. Find out what you wish to be or do, then train yourself for it. What you have undeveloped in you has no value. No one else either wishes or has the time to develop it. Set your eyes on a goal, and then fight for it. There must be an objective; set your compass and sail for that star when you find that objective. You must build a road to market your abilities. There is pain and fatigue ahead for you, but you dress for the job. Associate with the people who have won, those who will help you climb to the top. Don't hang around with a group of "have-beens" Associate with the men who are climbing up. The idle gossiping people will not help you; they will stand in your way. Put your money and time where it will pay you interest. This battle is not for the thoughtless, heedless guesser, or idealistic dreamer. Compel yourself to improve your mindset and your natural abilities. Cultivate discontent with everything ordinary in you and create them to extraordinary.

You are the best of anything that has existed on earth; your calling should not be traded for anything less. The consciousness of who you are enables you to maximize your potential in everything. You are not subject to the rules and procedures of this world or anybody. From the day you became a recreated spirit, God gave you a new beginning and His ability to become the best of you that you could be. Don't compromise your birthright for the mere porridge that Esau went for. You cannot get a victory in anything by dealing with the surface. You are a container of breath that tells your giants to a fall.

Many believers lose their spiritual credibility and authority for only temporary personal gains. When we trust and have faith in God, our phobias, complexes, and weaknesses are significantly reduced.

Matthew 10:16 Behold, I send you out as sheep in the midst of wolves. Therefore be wise as serpents and harmless as doves.

Mind-control and manipulation began with Satan when he induced one-third of the angelic host to rebel against God. Satan controls and manipulates human minds that are no match for angelic intelligence. The Devil uses the concept of fear as a weapon. Your mind has a direct relationship with one's spiritual choices.

2 Timothy 1:7 For God has not given us a spirit of fear but of power and of love and a sound mind.

The word of God is not a media construct or literature but a supernatural reality with the power to create and recreate changes, heal, provoke, mend, comfort, and reassure. Transformation enables you to discover your authentic self. God has the keys; whoever has the keys has the ability and power. God has the keys to your identity, and He is the best; once you have the best, you cannot go for the fake.

Our task might be to learn to understand God's will better, and if suffering comes our way, we might receive lessons that we thought were right in our view but might have been wrong in God's view. Prophesy is a part of our ability. Prophesy means to speak words that have potency, words that have divine power, and life to cause things to change. When you prophesy, you are not speaking empty words but words that can bring life and change ugly situations.

Fill your ear, eyes, and mouth with God's word so you can effect changes. If you cannot guard your territory, someone else will come and rule and run your territory, manipulate, and remote control your mind. The only way to know the answers to your problem is to know the man who reveals and does hold answers to your problems, the person of the Holy Spirit, He is your ability, and you cannot function in the spirit realm without Him.

The indwelling of the Holy Ghost in you causes you to have a new regenerating life; without the Holy Spirit, you cannot have a deep personal commitment to God, evidenced by your lifestyle. The deeper you travel in grace, the more it amazes you, the further you explore adoption, and the more you become lost in wonder and awe.

Acts 1:8 But you shall receive power when the Holy Spirit

has come upon you; and you shall be witnesses to Me in Jerusalem and in all Judea and Samaria and to the end of the earth.

God's adoption of us in Christ is legally binding. The Father takes an amazing step of sharing His own spirit with us.

2 Corinthians 4:6-7 For it is the God who commanded light to shine out of darkness, who has shone in our hearts to give the light of knowledge of the glory of God in the face of Jesus Christ vs7 But we have this treasure in earthen vessels that the excellence of power may be of God and not of us.

WHAT IS YOUR WORTH?

What value do you place on yourself? Have you ever taken an inventory or have you a sense of "I can do it if I want." Honestly, are you worth anything in your estimation? Have you set a price for your worth, ability, and time? Have your faith in your word? I am not asking what your word is worth outside; pride may make you keep your word with people, but do you keep your word with yourself? Set up your mark, your high standard. Take an inventory again and again and see what you possess; see whether that possession is more valuable today than it was a year ago.

Find where your ability lies, then put all your best into that ability, make that ability come across, and put you over to a higher frequency. Whatever you have hungered and yearned to do, you can do that if only you will. Make yourself a wanted person. Be so valuable that if you had to move, men and women would weep because of your departure. Harness that lazy mind and make it work. It is a value that counts in our Lord's final consideration of earthly ministry and life. What is your value? What is your impact? Indeed, not your cars, houses, education, or the number of children but your impact on God's kingdom. Your values represent what matters most to you. What is your value? Do you value God or the world and what it offers than your creator? The things you value affect every aspect of the way you interact with God and the world. What you value is who you become.

The spiritual failure is one who is born of God but refuses to develop and who has remained in an infant state for many years because of malnutrition. They feed upon the theories of men rather than upon the word of God. They live in the realm of sense knowledge rather than the realm of God's word. They are ever praying and asking God for faith, not realizing that all things belong to them,

2 Peter 1:3 His divine power hath given unto us all things that pertain unto life and godliness through the knowledge of him that hath called us to glory and virtue."

He has blessed us with every spiritual blessing in the heavenly places in Christ, and at the very beginning, God marked us out for the position of sons and daughters through Christ

Jesus unto Himself. Ephesians 1:3-4.

The purpose of God is to have healthy and vigorous children; He does not take pleasure in having us sick, mentally, physically, and spiritually.

Life is a checkerboard, and the player opposite you is time. If you hesitate before moving forward, grow or neglect to move promptly, your folks will wipe off the board in time. You are playing against a partner who will not tolerate indecision, and that partner is time. When you are super-saturated with the conviction that Jesus is Lord of all, this conviction controls your attitude, how you talk, what you hear, and what you think makes you valuable to God.

A man cannot be in Christ and have the devil's nature in him. He is either in the family of God or in the family of Satan.

1 John 3:10 "In this the children of God are manifest, and the children of the devil." There can be no real growth and development of faith, no strong, victorious Christian life with mixed conception. If you live a life of weakness and defeat, you do not know what and who you are in Christ.

Colossians 1:21-22, "Being in time past alienated and enemies in your mind in your evil works, yet now hath he reconciled in the body of His flesh through death to present you holy and without blemish and unreprovable before him."

Until a man is righteous and knows it, Satan reigns over him;

sin and diseases are his masters. But the instant he knows that he is the righteousness of God in Christ and knows what that righteousness means, Satan is defeated.

God's redemption in Christ is the solution. It makes a man a dominant spirit where he has served as a slave in weakness. His righteousness comes to you by talking to Jesus Christ as Savior and confessing His Lordship over your life.

2 Corinthians 5:21 "Him who knew no sin God made to become sin on our behalf; that we might become the righteousness of God in him."

This is the nature of God imparted to you. It is that nature gaining the ascendency in you until you know that you are what God says you are - masters, conquerors, and overcomers. Unless you are ready to do the impossible, you will never come into maternity (Growth and winning souls to birth). You have clothing that is not made on earth. Your whole nature must have a clothing of all righteousness. How great is the position of the man who is born of God, born of purity, born of faith, born of life, and born of power. You must bring your mind to the word of God and not bring the word of God to your mind. Those who walk with God always reach their destination.

YOU ARE A PARTAKER OF THE FULLNESS OF GOD IN CHRIST:

God has wrought a redemption that covers every phase of man's need and perfectly restores his fellowship with the father so that there is no sense of guilt or sin, no memory of past wrongdoing. The believer stands complete in Christ. He has partaken of the fullness of God in Christ.

John 1:16 "For of His fullness have we all received and grace upon grace.

When you read the book of Hebrews 10:1-19, you will meticulously find under the first covenant, there was a remembrance made of sins year after year, but in the New Testament, a man who has accepted Jesus Christ loses the sense of sin and in its place receives an understanding of his oneness and fellowship with the Father.

Colossians 1:13-14 "Who has delivered us out of the authority of darkness and translated us into the Kingdom of the Son of his love; in whom we have our redemption, the remission of our sins."

There are four facts here; first, you are delivered out of Satan's dominion. Second, you are born into the kingdom of the Son of his love. The third is, *"In Whom we have our redemption,"* which is a redemption from the devil's dominion. Satan has no legal right to reign over the man who has accepted Christ as his saviour. That man has been delivered out of the devil's dominion, family, and authority. He has been born and translated into the family of God, the kingdom of the Son of His love. Fourth, He did not only redeem you out of Satan's dominion; instead, there is a remission of your sins. He redeems you; He recreates you. He delivers you out of Satan's authority and remits all you have done.

You are recreated to be like Christ on earth in all His performances, to reflect His purpose as He was on earth.

1 John 4:17 Love has been perfected among us in this: that we may have boldness in the Day of Judgment; because as He is, so are we in this world.

You are recreated in His footprints to work His works, talk His talks, and think His thoughts. And He has given you His ability through the Holy Ghost to enable you to work His footprints on the earth. Apostle Paul said, *"I can do all things through Christ who strengthens me."* That means He is your strength; you can work His footprints on earth through the delegated authority which is in His name. No wonder *Colossians 3:17 says, And whatever you do in word or deed, do all in the name of the Lord Jesus, giving thanks to God the Father through Him.*

Christ deposited His authority in you so you can work His footprints on the earth. The authority is in His Name, Jesus.

Philippians 2:9-10 Therefore God also has highly exalted Him and given Him the Name which is above every name vs10 that at the Name of Jesus every knee should bow, of those in heaven and of those on earth vs11 and that every tongue should confess that Jesus Christ is Lord, to the glory of God the Father.

The Bible tells you that you have the mind of Christ. You are recreated to think His thought, which is to do the will of the Father in heaven. To live His thoughts deposited into your spirit man as you journey in the word of God. When the word saturates you, you begin to think His thoughts, seeing the impossible as possible. Unless you are ready to do the impossible, you will never come into maternity, a place where you give birth and bring souls to birth in His kingdom, a place where you give birth to His discerning spirit, His wisdom, His knowledge, His righteousness, justification, and His kind of faith not yours.

Colossians 2:2-3 that their hearts may be encouraged, being knit together in love and attaining to all riches of the full assurance of understanding, to knowledge of the mystery of God, both of the Father and of Christ in whom are hidden all the treasures of wisdom and knowledge.

1 Corinthians 2:16 For "who has known the mind of the Lord that he may instruct Him? But we have the mind of Christ."

You are recreated to bring your mind to the word of God and Christ, who is His Word, and not to be conscious to bring the word of God to your mind. His mind is to do the will of the Father, and since you are recreated to have His mind, your mind should be to do the will of Father God in heaven. *Colossians 3:1 If then you were raised with Christ, seek those things which are above, where Christ is, sitting at the right hand of God.*

You have the aroma of Christ in your spirit man; you are not just a happenstance. When you are confronted with the onslaughts of the devil, the onslaughts and every ugly circumstance will smell the aroma of Christ in your spirit man. You become dangerous to every satanic attack if you carry the footprint of Christ in your spirit man.

2 Corinthians 2:14-17 Now thanks be to God who always leads us in triumph in Christ and through us diffuses the fragrances of His knowledge in every place, for we are to God the fragrance of Christ among those who are being saved and among those who are perishing To the one, we are the aroma of death leading to death and to the other the aroma of life leading to life. And who is sufficient for these things? For we are not, as so many, peddling the word of God; but as of sincerity, but as from God, we speak in the sight of God in Christ.

You are the aroma of death to the onslaughts of the enemy; when demographic onslaughts confront you, they die from electrocution, smelling your aroma which is the aroma of Christ deposited in your spirit man. You are an aroma of life when you speak hope to the hopeless when you speak and preach God's word, when you set those in bondage and captives free when you heal the sick and mend the broken hearted, when you take care of the poor, fatherless, widows, and motherless. Your aroma is not for peddling; the authority and abundance vested in you are not for material gains but in sincerity demonstrating the footprint of Christ deposited in your spirit man. You are called to do an exploit, to an inheritance, incorruptible and undefiled, and that does not fade away, reserved in heaven for you. 2 Peter 1:3-4 As His divine power has given to us all things that pertain to life and godliness, through the knowledge of Him who called us by glory and virtue vs4 by which have been given to us exceedingly great and precious promises that through these you may be partakers of the divine nature, having escaped the corruption that is in the world through lust.

When you became recreated, you inherited the divine nature of Christ and the precious promises, not only to live in abundance but also to do great exploit and escape the corrupted environment of the universe.

James 1:18 Of His will he brought us forth by the word of truth that we might be a kind of firstfruits of his creatures.

You are created extraordinary to be the first fruit, Christ-like in nature, not of your own merit but because it is the unconditional will of God to let you be so. God decided at His will to let you be his first fruit. You are recreated to act, and you grieve the Holy Ghost when you do not act your identity. Just as you have products made in factories of the world, made in Germany, made in Japan, made in China, made in the USA, made in Switzerland, made in Nigeria, and made in England, etc. So, God recreated you and put His seal on you, Made in Heaven, and as you walk the streets of the earth, every creature recognizes you, that you have a heavenly connection. Sickness, trials, depression, poverty, all see the seal of God on you.

Don't touch made in heaven. Recognize your identity because when you don't, every onslaught of the enemy will use your ignorance to keep you under bondage. You are the compass of your life, and the knowledge of who you are will make the wisdom of God become electricity in you, taking you from one higher frequency to another, from glory to glory.

Ephesians 4:30 And do not grieve the Holy Spirit of God, by whom you were sealed for the day of redemption.

CHAPTER 24

THE GARDEN OF EDEN IN YOUR HEART

Your personality has the power deposits to open many doors, but your character keeps the doors open. The Bible highlights that the Garden of Eden is rich with gold and other natural metals. (Genesis 2:11-12) The Garden means voluptuous living, physically and spiritually designed for humans to exercise dominion on. Just as the Garden of Eden was Adam and Eve's place of abundant supply and voluptuous living, so is man's heart. Depending on what you plant, the heart is soil that has the potential to create a great harvest. Your heart is your Garden of Eden, *"Keep your heart with all diligence, for out of it spring the issues of life."*

Proverbs 4:23. Out of your heart springs your Garden of Eden. To plant the word of God in your heart, you must speak it, confess it, and meditate on it daily. Speaking God's word is the way to get it into the soil of your heart. God's word will change your life by planting it in your heart; you cultivate it to produce the fruit of His promises. Become a gatekeeper of your mindset. Deal with negative emotions, which are a sense of powerlessness. Achieving godly character is the bedrock of living the Christian life.

Joshua 1:8 *"This book of the law shall not depart from your mouth, but you shall meditate on it day and night, that you may observe to do according to all that is written in it. For then, you will make your way prosperous."*

Your identity is in the word of God. The word is your manual to live up to your identity to its fullest potential. The word of God is the footprint that brings your identity to its destiny. You must plant, bring to prophecy, speak, and talk the promises of God and locate your identity. You live in a word-created, word-controlled environment. Words are spiritual containers that carry faith or fear, blessing, or cursing, and they take shape in the realm of the spirit. Choose the right words to live up to the potent deposits in your spirit man.

Genesis 1:3 Then God said, "Let there be light," and there was light. Consistency in doing the things you know to do, such as prayer, studying and confessing the word, and spending time with God, is vital to unlocking your destiny. Developing character is a process that takes a while. You can't skip important stages of spiritual development on your road to your destiny. Preparation is the key to receiving the blessings and promises of God. Your identity can prepare your destiny. Even when it seems that things are not happening quickly, your identity will still take you through your destiny. Remain focused, cave in, and don't give up; life's pressures and challenges will forge God's character in you as you learn and depend on His word. In hard and good times, display a godly character by walking in love and allowing the fruit of the Spirit to be demonstrated and be supersaturated in your life.

It is the depths that God gets into that may reflect Him and manifest a life having Christ enthroned in the heart, drinking into a new fullness, a new intuition for as He is, so are we in this world. The Lord is the great promoter of divine possibility, pressing you into the attitude of daring to believe, "all things are possible if you believe."

If you find out who you are, you will discover your destiny. The discovery of your identity is a prelude to finding your destiny. What is your purpose? What are you put on earth to do? Unfortunately, folks go through life struggles, never accomplishing what they were put here to do. They end up living empty, frustrating existence.

God wants you to have a job to pay your bills and take care of your family and needs; working a nine-to-five job and retiring when you are sixty-five is not God's definition of a fulfilling life. Your job is not your source. It is a way for you to have money to sow into the kingdom of God so that you can increase. God doesn't want you to be dependent solely on your job to make it. He has a higher and greater plan for your life, and it is up to you to discover that plan. Your success is connected to your identity; your success in life is directly connected to your purpose and destiny. God has something specific for you to do. He deposits certain gifts and abilities inside you that He wants you to reach others. When you are walking in God's purpose for your life, you have located your identity and are fulfilling your destiny. Fulfillment is assured when you are walking in your purpose and destiny.

If your "Persona" becomes bigger than your person, it will kill who you are, your identity. If you allow people, no matter who they are, to make more withdrawals than deposits in your life, you will be out of balance and in the negative. Haters are people who will broadcast your failures and whisper your success

THE HEART WHERE YOUR TREASURE IS:

Proverbs 4:23 Keep your heart with all diligence, for out of it spring the issues of life.

Many folks have lost out because their minds prevent them from letting God reach their hearts. It is with the heart we believe unto righteousness; it is the heart where we believe in faith; it is the heart that is inhabited by the spirit. It is the heart that is moved by God. The mind is secondary. The heart conceives, the mind reflects, and the mouth is operated. The heart believes, like a ventilator, that it flows through and quickens the members of the mind. Then the tongue speaks of the glory of the Lord. It is an extraordinary experience to be in a great position to be saved by the immensity of power, the great inflow of life which is in the great fullness of God. *John 1:16 "And of His fullness we have all received and grace to grace."* You are enveloped by the wonderful inhabiting of the Holy Ghost, who comes right into your human soul, shakes the husks and ugly circumstances, and gives you a vision through the revelation.

YOU'RE PERSON IN SONSHIP:

A pin of truth leads you to a place of the sovereignty of purity, where any situation cannot move you. You have a fixed position on the authority of the word of Jesus Christ.

1 John 3:1 "Behold what manner of love the Father has bestowed on us, that we should be called children of God."

It is one of those manifold expressions. It is God who looks past your weakness and human depravities; all your makeup, which you know was out of order, and He has washed you, cleansed you, and beautified you. You are lovely. The world knows us not in our sonship.

Galatians 4:6 And because you are sons, God has sent forth the Spirit of His Son into your hearts, crying "Abba, Father" Take the stand, come into line and say, "I will be that Jesus proclaimed in John 10:36; I am the Son of God."

Luke 7:35, "But wisdom is justified by all her children." It is the will of God to choose you, it is not your choice, it the Lord's choice.

1 John 3:2 "Beloved, now we are children of God, and it has not yet been revealed what we shall be, but we know that when he is revealed, we shall be like Him, for we shall see Him as He is."

This is the life in a believer and a believer's consciousness to dwell and walk-through life's ups and down in this consciousness. Everyone who has this hope indwelling in him will work out his salvation.

1 John 3:3 "And everyone who has this hope in Him purifies himself, just as He is pure."

This is the hope of sonship, the hope of ministry, and the hope of life.

Difficulty rises and brings perplexity because we do not see that the Lord is greater than all. Observance comes from an inward holy flame kindled by God. God has done something extraordinary for the believer in that He has taken him out of the world.

"I do not pray that you should take them out of the world---They are not of the world" (John 17:15-16). Apostle Paul knew Jesus by revelation. He did not know Him from being with Him in His human nature and ministry as other apostles did. All Paul wanted after the revelation was to gain an increasing faith, and so he was always pressing on and wanted to remove every hindrance and interference.

John 6:38-40 "For I have come down from heaven, not to do My own will but the will of Him who sent Me. "This is the will of the Father who sent Me, that of all He has given Me I should lose nothing but should raise it up at the last day.

"And this is the will of Him who sent Me, that everyone who sees the Son and believes in Him may have everlasting life; and I will raise him up at the last day."

There is a need to apprehend your apprehension. God's word is your strength; your needs will not be met if you do not edify yourself with it. Always be watchful for divine inspirations.

Jesus came to do His Father's will, and as co-son with Jesus, you are planted here on earth to do the Father's will as Jesus did.

"For whosoever shall do the will of my Father in heaven is brother and sister and mother. (Matthew 12:50)

Jesus Christ was specific in recognizing those who are co-sons with Him by defining the purpose and vision of those who will share in the sonship as being doers of the Father's will.

The sense of mastery, the strange new dignity of sonship, sweeps over our hearts. You comprehend what it means to be under orders from heaven. You are clothed with authority from heaven.

You never get into a new place until you leave the old one. You must model God's personality. Jesus identified Himself with us as First fruit. "But each one in his order; Christ the first fruits, afterward those who are Christ's at His coming. (1 Corinthians 15:23).

You are a co-son and first fruit with Jesus Christ. "Of His own will He brought us forth by the word of truth, that we might be a kind of firstfruits of His creatures." (James 1:18) *Galatians 3:26-27 "For you are all sons of God through faith in Christ Jesus vs27 For as many of you as were baptized into Christ have put on Christ."*

CHAPTER 25

INCARNATION OF MAN

Romans 8:1-2 "There is no condemnation to those who are in Christ Jesus, who do not walk according to the flesh, but according to the spirit vs2 For the law of the Spirit of life in Christ Jesus has made me free from the law of sin and death."

The natural man has a highly developed sin consciousness, a spirit inferiority complex, and a sense of unworthiness that dominates him. He is ruled by doubt. All he has is a sense of knowledge and faith that he cannot know God or find him. The feeling of self-condemnation has given man an inferiority complex that makes him a coward. It robs him of faith in himself, man, God, and His word. This sin consciousness holds him in bondage; he thinks he has no right to approach God and believes he is not good enough to pray and have his prayers answered. This leads him to philosophy; he can no more keep away from the subject of God and religion than a hungry man can keep away from food.

This sense of guilt, inferiority, failure, and weakness makes him reason, and that reasoning is philosophy. The primary thing is that if you are without condemnation, you are in a place where you can pray through. You can have a revelation of Christ. For Christ to be in you brings you to a place where you cannot, if you follow the commands and leadings of the Spirit of Christ, have any fellowship with the world. It is the Spirit alone that by revelation brings the whole truth, visiting the Son in your hearts and revealing to you the capabilities of sonship that are in you after you are recreated. To be filled with God means that you are free. You are filled with joy, peace, blessings, and strength of character. You are transformed by God's mighty power.

There are two kinds of laws here, "The law of the Spirit of life in Christ," and the "law of sin and death." The law of the Spirit of life makes you free from the law of sin and death. The law of sin and death is in you as it was before, but it is dead. You still have your flesh, but its power over you is limited. You are the same person but have been awakened into a higher spiritual life and frequency; you must reign, and God made you like Him, so you must reign.

God has a plan beyond anything that we have ever known. He has a plan for every individual life; if we have any other plan in view, we miss the grandest plan. Nothing in the past is equal to the present, and nothing in the present can equal the things of tomorrow. Tomorrow should be so filled with holy expectations that we will be living flames for God. God never intended His people to be ordinary, commonplace, or second-hand. He intended that we should be on fire for Him, conscious of His divine power, realizing the glory of the cross that foreshadows the crown.

EPISTLE OF GOD:

2 Corinthians 3:3-4 clearly you are an epistle of Christ, ministered by us, written not with ink but by the Spirit of the living God, not on tablets of stone but on tablets of flesh, that is of the heart, And we have such trust through Christ toward God.

There is no way Christ can live in you except by the manifested word in you, through you, manifestly declaring every day that you are a living epistle of God. No man is perfect or equipped in any area except as the living word abides in him. The word is the living Christ, it is the divine likeness to God, and it is the express image of him. The word is the only factor that works out and brings forth in you, the glories of identification between you and Christ. *"Let the word of Christ dwell in you richly in all wisdom, teaching and admonishing one another in Psalms and hymns and spiritual songs with grace in your hearts to the Lord. (Colossians 3:16).*

We reign as kings in the realm of life through Jesus Christ. We begin to understand *1 Corinthians 12:3 "And no man can say, Jesus is Lord but in the Holy Spirit."*

When Jesus said, "All authority has been given to Me in heaven and on earth," that was for the church and this dispensation. That authority was not for Jesus but for you. His Name made you free from condemnation, free from satanic dominion, by redemption, and by your New Creation. In Christ, dominion was restored to the church. It is restored in the name of Jesus. The lost authority was invested in Christ. Go therefore and use this authority. He gave you the legal right to use His Name, the power of attorney; He bids you to come boldly to the throne room, to the throne of grace, and make your requests known. You are not to come there as an enslaved person or as a servant. You come as a son. In Pauline revelation, you are in the mind of the Father and in the mind of the Master, a son or daughter with limitless possibilities in the New Covenant and in your relationship with Him as a son and as a daughter. Dominion has been restored to you.

Do not live a mediocre life when you should be a superman.

Ephesians 2.10 "For we are His workmanship, created in Christ Jesus, for good works, which God prepared beforehand that we should walk in them."

You are His epistle created to manifest good works and exercise dominion invested in you through Christ. If one is free from the sense of guilt and condemnation, faith grows into miracle-working power. *"The works that I do shall you do also and greater works than these he will do" (John 14:12).*

The life from the Spirit's realm changes that which could not be changed, the impossible. Only the expression of the nature of God moving in your human faculty makes you know that you are begotten from heaven, changed by His power, transformed by His love. The grace has come upon you to transform your fashion and beautify your comeliness till all within you become an expression of the glory of God. You are a carrier of blessed privileges. Your natural capability cannot qualify you for a divine task or inheritance. Divine assignments require divine identity and strength; divine strength can only be made perfect in weakness.

2 Corinthians 12:9 And he said unto me, my grace is sufficient for you; for My strength is made perfect in weakness, most gladly therefore will I rather glory in my infirmities that the power of Christ may rest upon me.

Never allow someone to be your priority while allowing yourself to be their option. Refuse to allow someone's insecurity to be projected on you. Someone's insecurity is not an indication of your insecurity. There is a glory where you forget your poverties, your weaknesses, your human nature history, and you go to the divine opportunity.

CHAPTER 26

SMALL THINGS THAT CAN MAKE YOU LOSE GOD'S BIG

Jude 1:22-25 And some has compassion making a difference. And others save with fear, pulling them out of the fire; hating even the garment sported by the flesh. Now unto Him that is able to keep you from failing and to present you faultless before the presence of His glory with exceeding joy. To the only wise God our Savior be glory and majesty, dominion and power, both now and forever Amen.

When you voice out your faith, you give power to your spirit. When you train the sensitivity of your spirit, your spirit takes charge and drowns your fear. Fear is a purulent matter, it discharges pus. Christianity is a supernatural walk with God.

You build a spiritually sensitive spirit by studying and understanding the word of God. Acting on the word quickly by responding to the word quickly, you condition yourself to the lordship of the word in your life. God is not going to do for you what you can do for yourself. The longer you wait, the more difficult it becomes to overcome. There must be a significant shift for the better to happen. Jealousy is a small thing to keep you away from your destiny. Don't let something small keep you away from God's big. Nourish your identity to be in line with God's word.

What you cannot see is on the other side of the mountain, healing, prosperity, promotion, edification, joy, and peace. Obedience is the transport channel to the other side of the mountain. Do not miss something great because you are eying the little or because of pushing something down.

Part of your flesh must go lower any time you go higher. Starve the flesh and feed the spirit; the pain of discipline is temporal. Having a plan causes your vision to be more in tune. Having a clear vision makes your purpose clear. You must have a vision statement to accomplish your life's purpose. Being sensitive to the voice of the Holy Spirit will keep you from crashing. God keeps you because of the integrity of your heart. There must be something that stands between you and your destiny, pride, addiction, jealousy, hatred, or something small that makes you lose God's big.

THE HALLMARK OF DECISION-MAKING:

You are the compass of your life, God has given you

everything, but you must make your miracle happen. Your identity is supposed to carry you to where your treasures are.

Every decision-making has got its confrontations. Most of the time, you are hated, neglected, and called funny names for having made decisions that will bring you to your destiny. But if you ignore the confrontation and make some vital decisions, your identity will be profound.

Proverbs 24:7 &13-14 Wisdom is too high for a fool, He does not open his mouth in the gate vs13 my son eat honey (wisdom) because it is good. And honeycomb (knowledge) which is sweet to your taste so shall the knowledge of wisdom be to your soul. If you have found it, there is a prospect and your hope will not be cut off.

Resourceful decision-making changes your perception. It makes you walk taller, live better, and think higher. It changes you overwhelmingly, you become a well of joy unspeakable. Good decisions become Christ in you, the hope of all glory (Colossians 1:27).

Jesus Christ changes life and heart from a special place. He takes away pains when you involve Him in your decision-making; He comes into your life, and you begin to win every day. You will not walk the same when He is involved in your decisions. Your steps change, your mood changes, and your attitude becomes light in dark places.

Exposure and decision-making are vital keys to your success.

When you are exposed to things that give you options, options give you choices, and choices require decisions. The next step is to decide what you want to do.

Proverbs 4:7-9 Wisdom is the principal thing, therefore get wisdom. And in all your getting, get understanding. Exalt her (wisdom) and she (wisdom) will promote you. She (wisdom) will bring you honor. When you embrace her she will place on your head an ornament of grace. A crown of glory she will deliver to you.

Decision-making is the oxygen of life. It is a catalyst to your destiny when they are made by God's standard. If you consume your decision, its destiny is destroyed, but if you plant it, it becomes a tree. Move away from people who try to cultivate you, people who make you feel that your little is too nice. Get information before you make a decision. Information is your capital. If you want to build a house, get to know the cost; don't start a house you cannot finish.

Christianity is what I do with what I learn; it is not only words; it is practical. *1 Corinthians 4:20 "For the kingdom of God is not in word but in power."*

There are decisions that have a time frame; if you miss it at that particular time, you have destroyed your destiny. Some people are afraid to make decisions, they have been confronted with options for years, but they miss the opportunity for change because they chose not to change.

A decision is like an earthquake; it has consequences. It may affect your whole mental life or refresh your present standing. There are decisions you make with the information, and there are ones you make with revelation. Certain things you pray for need no prayer but your decision. Everything that has to do with the five physical senses- sight, smell, feeling, touch, and taste is decision-oriented. If you want to go to the toilet, you need no prayers but the decision, and if you ignore the decision and start to pray, you might be in for the biggest mess. A decision is the root cause of your troubles and problems. It is a confrontation between your destiny and success. The only decision God talks to you about are predestinated decisions that come through revelation. You must stop asking God questions that have nothing to do with your destiny. He will not tell you what to wear to church on Sunday or what to eat after work, this is the reason a Christian must have a changed mentality and identity.

Proverbs 3:5-6: Trust in the Lord with all your heart and lean not on your own understanding vs6 in all your ways acknowledge Him and He shall direct your paths.

When you make decisions based on human rationale instead of divine revelation or order, you distance yourself from the blessings and promises of God. Life is a constant struggle between good and evil, right, and wrong, God's way and the w world's waye must all make choices and decide what we want.

2 Corinthians 1:12 Now this our boast: our conscience testifies that we have conducted ourselves in the world and especially in our relation with you, in holiness and sincerity that are from God. We have done so not according to worldly wisdom but according to God's grace.

Proverbs 12:15 The way of a fool seems right to him but a wise man listens to advice. Everything looks small compared to God, who reveals Himself layer by layer, power by power. When you spend time with God, you will have a bigger view of who He is and empowering view of who you are towards everything that confronts you.

The daily choice starts with self-denial, choosing to honour God with your day rather than self-applause to yourself and the people around you. Concentrate on what God thinks and says about you and what He says about you being a person of destiny. You are created to have a date with destiny.

Hebrews 11:32-34 and what more shall I say? For time would fail me to tell of Gideon and Barak and Samson and Jephthah, also of David and Samuel and the prophets who through faith subdued kingdoms, worked righteousness, obtained the promise, stopped the mouths of lions quenched the violence, of fire, escaped the edge of the sword, out of weakness were made strong, became valiant in battle, turned to fight the armies of the aliens.

Your decisions will affect the quality of your life. Faith enables you to choose God's plan over your own plan. Your faith based on God's promises helps you see that trying to improve God's plan by substituting your plan, leads to frustration and problems. Your calling is to choose authenticity (trustworthy, undisputed origin) over prestige.

Moses gave up everything, all the prestige of a royal family, to secure his identity. He was adopted as the son of Pharaoh's daughter. He was in line to rule. So why did Moses throw away all that to identify with a Hebrew slave?

It was an encounter with God that changed Moses. God's children should neither bow down to Pharaoh and his demands nor sell their identity for a portion of pottage. When you have an encounter with God, you can never sell your identity for anything small; you have access to the original, and you cannot settle for the fake. We need to choose an authentic, honest relationship with God.

You need to have an attitudinal change, stocktaking, - a shift from prestige to choosing authenticity. In this, God becomes more prominent in your focus, as focus on self becomes less vital. The value of self-denial is the hallmark of Christianity. Self-discipline is a good thing. You must learn the art of self-denial because it produces spiritual strength and fitness. It was a personal relationship with God that changed Moses.

Moses feared Pharaoh at first, but after he went through God's training, Pharaoh became small in Moses' mind. Pharaoh's army was reduced, his wealth was reduced, and his little gods and magicians were all belittled in Moses' mindset.

To have a divine insight is to do and act the word of God. *James 1:22 "Be doers of the word"* means acting and confessing the dictates of the word of God revealed in the Bible irrespective of the circumstances or conditions around you. *Philippians 4:6-7 Be anxious for nothing but in everything by prayer and supplication, with thanksgiving, let your requests be made known to God vs7 and the peace of God which surpasses all understanding will guard your hearts and minds through Christ Jesus.*

When you are anxious, you are not doing the word or acting on the dictates of the word. Do not be anxious when you make decisions. It is not in your nature to be anxious. God is showing you your image and identity. It is not a commandment because your nature is devoid of worry.

Don't tell God what you are going through because He is not interested, but He is only interested in what you want. So, tell Him what you want. God does not respond to complaints because He is a Solution: that's why complainers don't win.

Revelation 1:6 And hath made us kings and priest unto God and His Father, to Him be glory and dominion forever and ever. Amen.

When we sit together as kings, it is a fraternity (developed from having common interests) and association of divinity.

We discuss kingdom purposes and divine promises. We discuss what we want and not what we are going through. When we make a request, the peace of God keeps us. *And the peace of God, which surpasses all understanding, will guard your hearts and minds through Christ Jesus. (Philippians 4:7)*

Every situation you find yourself in was made for a trophy. Every problem you have was built for a testimony. *James 5:13 Is any one in trouble? He should pray. Is anyone happy? Let him sing songs of praise (NIV).*

This portion did not say complain but pray, request and demand. God wants to come into your circumstance, no matter how your circumstance has enveloped you. He wants to have a personal encounter with you in your desert places so that your circumstance will produce the gift of faith. By the gift of faith, nothing shall be impossible. God does not do anything except by plan. You need to plan to meet God's plan so that His divine purpose for your life will flourish. Draw a line of your past so that you can open a new chapter and step into a new incredible dimension. Step into a new dispensation and a new beginning.

Jeremiah 29:11-13 For I know the thoughts that I think toward you, says the Lord, thoughts of peace and not of evil, to give you a future and a hope. Then you will call upon Me and I will listen to you And you will seek Me and find Me, when you search for Me with all your heart.

When you acknowledge the sovereignty of God in your life, every stronghold becomes a freehold; anything that keeps you from excelling in your area of talents and skills are destroyed. Every lazy element in your life is made strong. Enlarge your coast and have dominion. This is the code of your identity. God is the only true stable God that exists. Success is never final, and failure is never fatal. It is your courage that counts. The best antidote for fear is the word of God. You can only grow in grace by practicing putting your faith in God to work and receiving his grace in difficult situations.

Psalm 50:15 Call upon Me in the day of trouble; I will deliver you and you shall glorify Me.

CHAPTER 27

WISDOM IS IN YOUR DESTINY

WISDOM IS IN YOUR DESTINY:

James 1:5 If any of you lacks wisdom, let him ask of God who gives to all liberally and without reproach and it will be given to him.

The wisdom talked about here is called Sophia in Greek, which is the insight God gives you into the reality of all knowledge beyond science.

This wisdom in Christ is a pearl granted when you become born again, born into the family of God, deposited in your spirit man. The ordinary mind does not understand this wisdom or its chemistry.

If you have God's ability and God's wisdom, and you let

them loose, what limitlessness will there be to your ministry? It is not a problem of education but of God loosen in you, liberating the ability of God within you. Enclosed in you today is the ability of God. Jesus Christ has supersaturated you with wisdom. He has been made unto you wisdom. "But of Him are you in Christ Jesus, who was made unto us wisdom from God."

James told the babes in Christ that if they lacked wisdom, they could ask for it from God.

James 1:5-8) (Weymouth) *"And if any one of you is deficient in wisdom, let him ask for it, who gives with open hand to all men and without upbraiding; and it will be given him. But let him ask in faith and have no doubt, for he who doubts is like the surge of the sea driven by the wind and tossed into spray. A person of that sort must not expect to receive anything from the Lord, such one is man of two minds, undecided in every step he takes.*

You are grown up now. You have passed the period of *babyhood*, and now you know that Jesus is your wisdom. Wisdom is the ability to use knowledge. You have the knowledge of the life of God in you. You have the knowledge of the power and authority of the word. You have the knowledge of your legal right to use the name of Jesus in your combat operation with spiritual forces. You have the knowledge of the fact that God is actually in your body.

You have the power of attorney to use these mighty facts to bless humanity. God has set you free *(John 8:36)*. *"If the son therefore shall make you free, you shall be free indeed"* You are no longer hidden, people know who you are. You have let God loose in you and have given Him His liberty to heal the sick, to bless the world.

Colossians 2:2 -4 That their hearts be encouraged, being knit together in love and attaining to all riches of the full assurance of understanding, to the knowledge of the mystery of God, both of the father and of Christ. In whom are hidden all the treasures of wisdom and knowledge vs4 Now this I say lest anyone deceive you.

Ephesians 3: 9-13 And to make all see what is the fellowship of the mystery which from the beginning of the ages has been hidden in God who created all things through Jesus Christ vs10 to the intent that now the manifold wisdom of God might be made known by the church to the principalities and powers in the heavenly places according to the eternal purpose which He accomplished in Christ Jesus our Lord. In whom we have boldness and access with confidence through faith in Him. Therefore I ask that you do not lose heart at my tribulation for you, which is your glory.

Worldly wisdom is the ability or result of an ability or an act utilizing knowledge, experience, understanding, common sense and insight, and accumulation of knowledge. The ability to discern or judge what is true, right, wrong, or lasting insight.

1 Corinthians 3:19-21 For the wisdom of this world is foolishness with God. For it is written, "He catches the wise in their own craftiness" and again," The Lord knows the thoughts of the wise, that they are futile. Therefore let no one boast in men. For all things are yours.

The fear of God is the beginning of wisdom; when you fear and have a consistent intimacy with God and walk in fellowship with Him, you are in line. The scope of your wisdom can be measured within the intimacy. The more you grow in His grace, the more wisdom you acquire from Him. Your frequencies become higher, and you take a consistent walk with Him.

Proverbs 1:7 the fear of the Lord is the beginning of knowledge but fools despise wisdom and instruction.

You should live in the consciousness of wisdom deposited in your spirit man because wisdom is highly valued; it is a principal thing that stirs you up and makes you make wise choices.

Proverbs 4:7 Wisdom is the principal thing. Therefore get wisdom. And in all your getting, get understanding.

The reason the enemy traps many Christians is because of wisdom; they are ignorant of the Sophia wisdom deposited in their spirit. They walk the earth in worldly wisdom, which is void of the understanding of the spiritual realm. The worldly wisdom cannot understand the things of God and cannot comprehend the chemistry.

Hosea 4:6 My people are destroyed for lack of knowledge. Because you have rejected knowledge, I also will reject you from being a priest for Me because you have forgotten the law of your God. I also will forget your children.

When you understand that you are born at conception with the wisdom of God deposited in your spirit, you act and demonstrate it. You begin to speak the wisdom of God in esoteric language.

You speak mystery, and this is not a language everybody comprehends. Your rank on earth does not matter. What matters is your rank in heaven, and that's why some of you are used as colonels and some Generals. Without God's wisdom, you cannot do any exploits here on earth. His wisdom will help you discern your spiritual walk on earth.

God must bring us to a place where we do not have merely a name but where we have the position that brings the name. You cannot know the mind of the natural and the mysteries of the hidden things with God unless power penetrates everything between you and heaven. The vision of Christ is so seen that you will have a measure that it will take all that God has for you. There is nothing that will profit you or bring you to a place of blessing except that which denounces or brings to death the natural order so that the supernatural plan of God may be in perfect order in you. The word is the only factor that works out and brings forth in you these glories of identification between you and Christ.

A personal acquaintance with the Lord Jesus by the revelation of the Spirit can so move you that in an instant, you may have the revelation that would cause you to see that an enthronement or wisdom now encases you from on high. You have an extravagant God with extravagant language to make you an extravagant person in wisdom. But extravagance without wisdom, will not profit you.

CHAPTER 28

PHYSICAL BUT LIVING IN THE SUPERNATURAL

To live below the supernatural is to engage in a fruitless journey to your destiny. To live in the supernatural is to live beyond what is physical. It is for a Christian to supersaturate his/ her life by living and walking in accordance with the dictates of God through the nurture of his spirit man in God's word. It is living and using God's word to take things from the spiritual realm and manifest them in the physical.

If you want to change your life to a meaningful one, change what you are talking about, change what you are seeing and what you hear every day. Principles control this world, and principles make life predictable. Predictably, you are not an accident here on earth; you have a purpose.

The scope of your possession is defined by revelation.

Genesis 12:1-3 now the Lord had said to Abram: "Get out of your country, from your family and from your father's house to a land that I will show you."

The critical factors here are revelation and obedience. That God revealed Himself to Abram and he obeyed are the scope of his possession. There is no durable future in position, there is none in location, but your future is in revelation.

Hebrews 11:6 But without faith, it is impossible to please Him, for he who comes to God must believe that He is and that He is a rewarder of those who diligently seek Him.

The scope of your possession is defined by revelation- what God has said to you and, your response and how you handle it.

Revelation is a personal affair; what you see is what you get. *Genesis 3:14-15 And the Lord said to Abram, after Lot had separated from him, "Lift your eyes and look from the place where you are-northward, southward, eastward and westward. "For all the land which you see I give to you and your descendants forever.*

Getting a revelation is a matter of personal responsibility. When you have a revelation, it gives you a voice. If you don't have a revelation, you are only an echo; you echo somebody else revelation. The scope of your possession is defined by your own revelation. Your life has been planned already by God. He planned the universe, and you have a portion. The guarantee of your possession is the Blood covenant- the certainty that God's promise will be fulfilled in your life.

Psalm 137:1-4 by the rivers of Babylon, there we sat down, yea we wept, when we remembered Zion how shall we sing the Lord's song in a strange town?

If there is any place to sing the Lord's song, it will be in a strange land. When you are jobless, when you are depressed, when you have no hope, when you are sick, when you have no money, these are your strange land, and it is the best time to sing the Lord's song.

God gave us the capacity for memory, to remember, but when the enemy steps in, he makes you focus on the negative, and he will not allow you to see what God has done; he will not allow you to sing the Lord's song in a strange land. It is natural to mourn when things are rough, but it is not spiritual. You don't know the secret to success until you know how to handle failure.

There is a difference between failure as a person and failure of an event. That your event failed does not make you a failure. *Genesis 1:26 says you are created in the image of God.* So, you cannot be a failure because God can never fail. You have the DNA of a winner, but you must keep trying and not give up; this is how to win. The part of you that was a failure died and was buried with Christ.

Romans 6:3-4 Or do you not know that as many of us as were baptized into Christ Jesus were baptized into His death vs4

Therefore we were buried with Him through baptism into death that just as Christ was raised from the dead by the glory of the Father, even so, we also should walk in newness of life.

It is not the things that happen to us that hurt us but how we respond to the things that happen that hurts us. Life depends on what you are seeing, you can choose to see what is not working, or you can choose to see what God is doing. Failure is not a failure but an opportunity to try again on a better note.

2 Corinthians 3:18 But we all, with unveiled face, beholding as in a mirror the glory of the Lord are being transformed into the same image from glory to glory, just as by the Spirit of the Lord.

What you focus on is what you are transformed into. Some people internalize their failure. They focus on failure until they become failures themselves. If your focus is on your mistakes, you become a mistake yourself.

Do not be possessed by the past but be forward-focused and forward-conscious. When you praise God in your strange land, He will raise you. Focus on what God is about to do because today and tomorrow will be better than yesterday.

Psalm 42:5-6 Why are you cast down, O my soul? And why are you disquieted within me? Hope in God, for I shall yet praise Him for the help of His countenance vs6 O, my God my soul is cast down within me, therefore I will remember You from the land of the Jordan and from the heights of Hermon from the hill Mizar.

Hopelessness is faithlessness. When you hang around God, that is when you know there is resurrection. John 12:24 say, *"Most assuredly, I say to you, unless a grain of wheat falls into the ground and dies, it remains alone; but if it dies, it produces much grain.*

Things do not die around God, but they die to live; the blessing is in the breaking.

Ecclesiastes 9:4a "But for him who is joined to all the living, there is hope."

Isaiah 6:1-3" The Spirit of the Lord God is upon Me, Because the Lord has anointed Me To preach good tidings to the poor; He has sent me to heal the brokenhearted; To proclaim liberty to the captives, And the opening of the prison to those who are bound vs2 To proclaim the acceptable year of the Lord; And the day of vengeance of our God; To comfort all who mourn vs3 To console those who mourn in Zion to give the beauty for ashes, to give the oil of joy for mourning, the garment of praise for the spirit of heaviness, that they may be called trees of righteousness, the planting of the Lord, that He may be glorified.

It is a dangerous thing to mourn in Zion- the Holy Spirit changes your identity before He changes your circumstance. *Psalm 23:3 "He restores my soul"*

If you are sorrowful, God cannot operate where you are. He cannot show up in the atmosphere of sorrow. Every human being is a magnet that has the potential to attract and the potential to repeal. The one, who is always sorrowful around God, repels His presence. The human system is not designed to harbor sorrow because you are the image of God. Sorrow is a choice; joy is a choice. No devil has a right to put a clown on your case unless you permit it, and neither give a place to the devil (Ephesians 4:27).

CHAPTER 29

CONFESSION IS THE LOCATION OF YOUR DESTINY

Joshua 1:8 This book of the law shall not depart out of thy <u>mouth;</u> but thou shall meditate therein day and night, that you may observe to do according to all that is written therein for then thou shall make thy way prosperous and then thou shall have good success.

Something to note here is that this portion did not say anything about the heart but that the word shall not depart from the mouth and not the heart. The heart cannot speak, but the mouth does. Those who say they mediate by heart should take note that the heart does not speak. It is the mouth that needs to speak the word of God consistently. To meditate means to mutter or say to yourself. Thinking is not meditation. Meditating means talking quietly or roaring aloud.

You may have the word in your heart, but if you don't speak

it forth to a situation, things don't change. Genesis Chapter one reveals that the world was a chaotic mass until God spoke. God has to speak to change things. You cannot have real Christianity by praying and singing in your mind.

Philemon 1:6 that the sharing of your faith may become effective by the acknowledging of every good thing which is in you in Christ Jesus.

To acknowledge in this context means speaking out your identity, speaking out about those things that you have been designed for by God Almighty.

Romans 10:8-10 But what does it say? "The word is near you, in your <u>mouth</u> and in your heart" that is the word of faith which we preach vs9 that if you confess with your <u>mouth</u> the Lord Jesus and believe in your heart that God raised Him from the dead, you will be saved vs10 For with the heart one believes unto righteousness and <u>with the mouth confession is made unto salvation.</u>

The mouth is a channel to reaching your destiny. The mouth is a transporter of divine purposes, inheritance, and promises to their manifold destination. The mouth was designed for confessions to come in the volume of what is written *"It is written."* No wonder the book of *Proverbs 18:21 says death and life are in the power of the tongue, and those who love it will eat its fruits.* The mouth has fruits; the mouth can also yield either deadly or divinely fruits, depending on how you use it.

Romans 10:6 But the righteousness of faith speaks in this way, "do not say in your heart, who will ascend into heaven? (That is to bring Christ down from above).

Faith and righteousness have a transporter; the mouth speaks faith and righteousness of Christ into manifestation. You are what you confess. Genesis 1:3 And God said, *"Let there be light and there was light."*

God reveals Himself to you through His word. This revelation alone wouldn't change the circumstances of your life; it has to become "Rhema," "the spoken word," the active and creative word in your mouth. The word of God on your lips is God talking. There are not enough limitations in the world to stop or hinder your progress if your mouth is consistently talking the word.

Job 22:28-29 Thou shalt also decree a thing and it shall be established unto thee; and the light shall shine upon thy ways vs29 When men are cast down, then thou shalt say, there is lifting up and he shall save the humble person.

Revelation 12:11 and they overcame him because of the Blood of the Lamb and because of the word of their testimony and they did not love their life even when faced with death.

Jeremiah 5:14 therefore thus says the Lord God of hosts: "Because you speak this word, Behold, I will make my words in your mouth fire, and this people wood, And it shall devour them.

When you speak the word of God, it becomes fire in your mouth. The word becomes a fire ready to address everything that raises its head against the will of God. The word becomes fire in your mouth and redresses every demographic onslaught of the enemy because you speak. When you speak the word of God consistently, you are dressed in the Mantle of God, and the Mantle is bigger than anointing; you can receive anointing through the laying of hands of a man. The Mantle is the Baptism of fire by the Holy Ghost. The Mantle is a direct laying of God's hands on you, it cannot be artificial, and the mantle is void of man's interference. The Mantle is for service, for confrontations. Glory to God, I have fire in my mouth because I speak His word.

THE WORD; THE ACCESS CODE:

Isaiah 61:1&4 The Spirit of the Lord God is upon me because the Lord has anointed me to preach good tidings to the poor. He has sent me to heal the brokenhearted, to proclaim liberty to the captives and the opening of the prison to those who are bound and they shall rebuild the old ruins. They shall raise up the former desolations. And they shall repair the ruined cities, the desolations of many generations.

Rhema is the Hebrew word for the word of God. You cannot be a safer Christian if you are not saturated with the word of God. The word of God in you activates the consciousness of who you are in Christ Jesus. The word of God will take you where the world cannot get you. It is the word of God that transforms you and transports and keeps you in the presence of God. The Bible says in His presence is the fullness of joy. You cannot withdraw your deposits in a world controlled by the enemy without your access code which is the word of God. The devil's mission is to keep you from hearing the word because he knows that when you have no deposits, you cannot withdraw in times of need. The devil knows when you are ignorant of God's word, you can do nothing. Apostle Paul was able to say in *Philippians 4:13 I can do all things through Christ who strengthens me.* The reason he took this stand was because of higher frequencies of the indwelling of God's word in him.

Hebrews 4:12 For the word of God is quick and powerful and sharper than any two edged sword, piercing even to the dividing asunder of soul and spirit and of joints and marrow and is a discerner of the thoughts and intents of the heart.

The word of God is not only an antidote or medicine for sickness and disease but also the perfect recipe for success and prosperity.

If you were sick and took time to meditate on the word, the word of God will produce healing in you. God's word is dependable, it is guaranteed to produce results, and it will deliver your inheritance into your hands. It does not matter the news that comes to you from afar; you are undisturbed.

Psalms 107:20 He sent His word and healed them and delivered them from their destructions.

Proverbs 4:20-22 My son, give attention to my words, incline your ear to my sayings. Do not let them depart from your eyes; keep them in the midst of your heart, for they are life to those who find them and health to all their flesh.

The word translated to health is the Hebrew word "marpe" which means medicine. The word of God is medicine to your physical body. It will rejuvenate and revitalize you when you apply it to your life. The word of God is alive and full of power. That means it is active, operative, and effective. It doesn't matter what life situation you are going through; if you hear the word of God concerning you, accept it, it will produce in you and for you the desired results.

God has sent His word already to address every situation you will ever face in life. He has sent His word for your deliverance, healing, prosperity, and spiritual advancement. It is your responsibility to lay hold of His word. The word of God in your spirit and your mouth will make you what it talks about. Therefore, you need to be all that God wants you to be and experience the divine transformation that will make you a wonder in your world.

Jeremiah 5:14 Therefore thus says the Lord god of Hosts, because you speak this word, Behold, I will make My words in your mouth fire and this people wood and it shall devour them.

The word of God has power and ability. God's word in your mouth produces harvest of what it talks about; it is fire against every wood that stays in opposition to your life; it consumes every sickness, poverty, joblessness, failure, depression, fear, and ungodliness. The word of God in your mouth is God-talking.

Isaiah 55:10-11 For as the rain comes down and the snow from heaven and do not return there but water the earth and make it bring forth and bud that it may give seed to the sower and bread to the eater v so shall My word be that goes forth from my mouth, it shall not return to me void but it shall accomplish what I please and it shall prosper in the thing which I sent it.

The most precious and influential people in the sight of God are soul winners who use His word to get people into the kingdom of God. God divinely protects them against evil and shields them from the attacks of the enemy. God kept you on earth because He has a lot of people He wants to reach through you.

Apostle Paul said in *1 Corinthians 9:16 For if I preach the gospel, I have nothing to boast of, for necessity is laid upon me, yes woe is me if I do not preach the gospel.* God has super protection for your life as you go about His business of reaching the lost through His word. God sees to your protection and prosperity and ensures you are successful in every area of your life.

God leads us to triumph through His word; it was the consciousness of his word that made David say to Goliath, "you come to me with a sword and with a spear and shield, but I come to thee in the name of the Lord of hosts, the God of the armies of Israel."

2 Corinthians 2:14 Now thanks be to God who always leads us in triumph in Christ and through us diffuses the fragrance of His knowledge in every place.

God held the sun and the moon in place at Joshua's word; in the same vein, when you decree anything in the name of Jesus, His power will back your word to make it happen. *John 14:14 says, "If you ask anything in my Name, I will do it and John 15:17 If you abide in Me and my words abide in you, you will ask what you desire and it shall be done for you.*

Prophecy is the illumination of the truth by the word of God. It is speaking the word and addressing situations. The Holy Spirit having the chief position in the place, taking words, acting everything till the word stands there completely. The

Holy Spirit is the oracle of God speaking words as if the Lord were saying them through our mouths.

There is such a wonderful display of wisdom and authority by the living word. Just as you become mindful on human lines, clothed upon with the word of God on divine lines, you shall be natural but supernatural, inwardly displaying the revelation of the power of God through your divine position.

Make the word of God a supernatural makeup overflowing full from you; the supernatural will always change the natural.

One word from the Lord is sufficient; one little word from God is all you require to change your circumstance. It will bring forth that which God has desired. God can tame your tongue; He can so reserve you for Himself that the whole of your body shall be in operation of the word.

God's spoken word is divinity that invades the vicinity and changes the stories of humanity. Prophecy is chosen and desired above faith, hope, charity, and above all the other gifts. The greatest amongst all is prophecy because prophecy by the power of the Spirit is the only power that saves humanity. The gospel brought through prophecy, has the power to bring immortality and light. Immortality is that which abides forever. Light opens the understanding of your heart. Everybody has the gift of speaking the word, and everybody has prophecy.

Revelation 19:10 And I fell at his feet to worship him, But he said to me, "see that you do not do that; I am your fellow servant and of your brethren who have the testimony of Jesus. Worship God; for the testimony of Jesus is the spirit of prophecy."

The word wants to know how they can be saved. Every one of you must be a preacher. You have a prophecy that comes from heaven to change you from vile inward corruption, transport your evil human nature, and put a spirit of testimony within you.

Make up your mind to be extraordinary by studying and speaking the word. Don't allow conventional thinking and beliefs dominate your environment or the failure of those before you to hinder your progress. Always use God's word to address your situations when they appear. When you constantly act on God's word, it causes circumstances to conform to His dictates. You will then accomplish the impossible and do the spectacular, reaching your peak in all your endeavours in the name of Jesus Christ and by the power of the Holy Ghost that inhabits you as you study God's word.

Psalm 119:8 &89 &103-105 &130 How can a young man cleanse his way? By taking heed according to Your word vs89 forever, O Lord, your word is settled in heaven vs103 how sweet are Your words to my taste, sweeter than honey to my mouth vs104 through Your precepts I get understanding. Therefore I hate every false way vs105 Your word is a lamp to my feet and a light to my path vs130 the entrance of Your words gives light. It gives understanding to the simple.

When the word of God supersaturates your chemistry, it compels you to act its dictates. You begin to reign in dominion to every life confrontation. You become a giant killer and a destiny changer because you speak words that change not only situations but also change destiny. Speaking the word enables you to locate your inheritance.

Acts 20:32 "So now, brethren, I commend you to God and to the word of His grace, which is able to build you up and give you an inheritance among all those who are sanctified.

There is always an increase in the spoken word of God; no word, no increase; no increase, no multiplication. *Acts 6:7 So the word spread, the number of disciples in Jerusalem increased rapidly and a large number of priests became obedient to the faith.*

CHAPTER 30

A POSSESSOR OF LEGAL VICTORY

You were created with a bounce-back potential. A bounce-back mentality is when you get knocked down, don't stay down, get back up again to fight. You cannot bounce back when you are busy celebrating a pity party. Self-pity destroys persuasion. God gives you double for your trouble because in your blood is the DNA of a winner. God has put a bounce back in your spirit because you have the seal of Christ on you.

There is a higher level where God wants to take you. He does not want you to remain stationary in your walk on earth. When God brings you to your higher level, He takes care of every spot, your finance, your job, your investment, your health, your mouth, your speech, your children, and everything in life.

He does not only give for yourself; he gives you for you

to share. You become a distributor of the gospel of life and grace. God made Abraham a connector, and you became a connector through Abraham so that you can connect with others. Anywhere you are, God put you there for a reason. There is a good fight to fight, the fight of faith. Until you overcome to the end, you will have the forces of the enemies working against you; some come in person and some in a group.

Joshua 1:6 "Be strong and of good courage, for to this people you shall divide as an inheritance the land which I swore to their fathers to give them."

If there is nothing to be strong about, God wouldn't have said to you be strong and of good courage. To divide any inheritance God has made available, you need to be strong and of good courage. You cannot convert spiritual blessings into material manifestations or physical reality if you lack courage and strength.

Hebrews 11:32-35 and what more shall I say? For the time would fail me to tell of Gideon and Barak and Samson and Jephthah, also of David and Samuel and the prophets who through faith subdued kingdoms, worked righteousness, obtained promises, stopped the mouths of lions, quenched the violence of fire, escaped the edge of the sword, out of weakness were made strong, became valiant in battle, turned to fight the armies of the aliens. Women receive their dead raised to life again; others were tortured, not accepting deliverance that they might obtain a better resurrection.

Your focus should not be on yourself when you go through suffering and trials; otherwise, you become a reservoir of pain and self-pity. God uses the pain you experience to equip you to encourage others in their trials. You are comforted to comfort others; you are completed not to complicate others but to complete them. Hence your miseries become your ministry. If you mourn over trouble, you will live in despair. The pains you go through in life will become wasted pain when you fail to learn from the pains you went through.

Psalm 144:1&3 Blessed be the Lord my Rock who trains my hands for war, and my fingers for battle. Lord what is man that You take knowledge of him? Or the son of man that You are mindful of him?

We speak the wisdom of God in esoteric language, in a language that not everybody understands but is designed for those who are heirs in the kingdom. Jesus has no natural competitor; there is no natural application in a spirit realm.

In *Mark 6:38 When Jesus wanted to feed the 5000, He asked the disciples "What do you have" and when the disciples brought the two loaves of bread and five fishes, Jesus broke them to abundance.*

Miracle begins with what you have. Miracles start with the recognition of what you have. It is the breaking of life that produces abundance. You need to be broken to handle and control God's abundance; what you have needs to be broken to attain your abundance. The blessing is in the breaking. You can be full of power and faith and will not demonstrate authority. The demonstration of authority manifests wonders and miracles and signs and wonders. Be a light in dark places.

Most of us are busy counting those we think are more important and significant than others, and we lose sight of the ones we regard as less significant but have the blessings and doors to the miracles. Don't let conventional thinking hold you back. Conventional thinking can destroy you, the source of your abundance.

Songs of Solomon 1:5-6 I am dark but beautiful, O girls of Jerusalem, tanned as the dark tents of Kadar but lovely as the silken tents of Solomon. Don't look down on me, you city girls, just because my complexion is so dark, the sun tanned me. My brothers were angry with me and sent me out into the sun to tend the vineyards but see what it has done to me (Living bible).

She had issues that turned her appearance dark. She has been through harsh life and conditions that would have made her bitter, ashamed, and unlovable, yet she didn't lose her self-value and worth. She realized that beauty is a mixture of physical, spiritual, and mental attributes. Have a strong sense of yourself and focus on your inner identity. You will find who holds your ability when you go through pains and suffering. Self-esteem is not what other people say about you but what you say about yourself through the volume of what is written and what God says about you. Let your eyes behold your beauty and speak it out loud to yourself.

Isaiah 40:28 Don't you yet understand? Don't you know by now that the everlasting God, the Creator of the farthest parts of the earth, never grows faint or weary? No one can fathom the depths of His understanding. He gives power to the tired and worn out and strength to the weak (Living Bible).

Progressing and regressing is always a matter of attitude and gratitude. Be thankful for what is not enough so the doors to what is enough can be open. Be grateful for what you don't have. Your mind is a canteen of possibility. Push until God responds, pushing is praying until something happens. Never give up; a loser gives up so soon.

Psalm 2:8 Ask of Me and I will give you the nations for your inheritance and the ends of the earth for your possession.

Practice does not make perfect. Perfect practice makes perfect. You will never get the level of training you need to become an overcomer when you engage in war games, when you don't saturate yourself with God's word, don't spend time in prayer, and don't sow seeds for the furtherance of the gospel. You cannot get something out of nothing. Isaiah 62:7 says, "And give God no rest until He establishes Jerusalem and makes her respected and admired through the earth" (Living Bible).

No soldier can rely on another soldier's rations, weapons,

or experience. Every soldier gets himself trained and armed for battle. Ensure you have the right tools and maintain the proper perspective and position. A soldier knows his or her position and rank. Prayer is a divine technology that when implemented, gives God permission to intervene in the affairs of humanity. Your life is framed and layout by the word of God. The life you live reflects your communication.

CHAPTER 31

THE CONSCIOUSNESS OF THE ENERGY IN YOU

John 1:9 & 5 That was the true light which gives light to every man coming into the world vs5 And the light shines in the darkness and the darkness did not comprehend it.

Matthew 5:14-16 You are the light of the world, a city on hill, glowing in the night for all to see. Don't hide your light. Let it shine for all; let your good deeds glow for all to see so that they will praise your heavenly Father (Living Bible).

God is Light, and you, as a believer, are also. Now there is strong chemistry between these two lights. One is a greater Light, and the other is the lesser light. The lesser light cannot function without the help of the greater Light.

2 Corinthians 4:6-7 For it is God who commanded light to shine out of darkness, who has shone in our hearts to give the light of the knowledge of the glory of god in face of Jesus Christ vs7 but we have this treasure in earthen vessels that the excellence of the power may be of God and not us.

God made the greater light to rule the day not just to shine in the day but to rule the day and there is also a lesser light to rule the night.

Genesis 1:14-18 Then god said, "Let there be lights in the firmament of the heavens to divide the day from the night and let them be for signs and seasons and for days and years and let them be for lights in the firmament of the heavens to give light on the earth and it was so then God made two great lights; the greater light to rule the day and the lesser light to rule the night, He made the stars also.

Psalm 136:4-9 To Him who alone does great things, for His mercy endures forever to Him who by wisdom made the heavens, for His mercy endures forever vs6 to Him who laid out the earth above the waters, for His mercy endures forever to Him who made great lights, for His mercy endures forever the sun to rule by day, for His mercy endures forever the moon and stars to rule by night, for His mercy endures forever.

The vital revelation about these two great lights is that one of them doesn't really have light of itself or by its own power. The moon doesn't have light itself. The moon shines from the light of the sun. It gets light from the sun, so it reflects its light from the sun. This means it really doesn't have its own light, so in a sense the moon is not a light. But it is a light by the power of the sun.

The word of God is a greater light "Thy word is a lamp unto my feet and alight unto my path" (Psalms 119:105) and "The entrance of thy words gives light; it gives understanding unto the simple (Psalm 119:130).

The light stands also for the truth. When you talk about greater and lesser lights, you are also talking about greater and lesser truth. If you got sick, this is the truth: that God would heal you, is a lesser truth. Because there is a greater truth, and the greater truth is that you are the son of God. "Now are we sons of God" this means you are a son of God now, that the spirit of God lives in you and has vitalized your mortal body. He says, "if the Spirit of Him that raised up Christ from the dead dwells in you, that same Spirit shall also vitalize your mortal body by His Spirit that lives in you." If God vitalizes your body, there is no place for sickness. The greater truth is that there shall be no sickness in the land. When you come into Christ, you come into a place called Zion, into the city of the living God, the heavenly Jerusalem.

These all happen now; you are an heir of God, and He says all things are yours. You may be asking God for money, a house, etc. These are the lesser truths when God ministers them to you. When you decree that it will happen, what you ask God: It is the lesser truth. There is a greater truth that declares that in the now of your life, all things are yours. It takes spiritual understanding to come to that point in your life where you function in the greater truth, and in the greater light. Your prayer life changes; you are not going to be asking, 'Oh God, make it possible for me to have this,' 'Oh God, make it possible for me to do this.' This is like asking God what already belongs to you; it is like trying to get what you already have. It is like journeying from a place where you are already coming from.

When you function in the frequency of the greater light, you begin to understand that your body is just your house where you dwell and that your body is not you, and not your identity. Your spirit takes dominion over your physical body because your body belongs to you, it is your house, you take dominion over it, and then you live a greater life.

Genesis 9:2 &7 "And the fear of you and the dread of you shall be on every beast of the earth on every bird of the air, on all that move on the earth and on all the fish of the sea. They are given into your hand. Vs 7 and as for you, be fruit and multiply. Bring forth abundantly in the earth and multiply.

Some folks say, "last year brought me a lot of troubles, and this year will bring me luck."

The reality is no year brings anything because the New Year is not a person. The year is an inanimate object; the year doesn't have intelligence and cannot bring something to you. The year was never made to bring something or anything to you. God never made you to have the year dictate the circumstances of your life.' We in our abilities should make something in the New Year to happen.

Ephesians 5:8 For you were once darkness but now you are light in the Lord. Walk as children of light.

Let your consciousness be "I am going to manifest that light in me" or "I am going to let my light shine" This means it is your responsibility to be a light in a dark world, to let your light shine in your new day, new month, and new year.

John 5:35 He was the burning and shining lamp and you were willing for a time to rejoice in his light. Jesus makes this declaration about john. He was a burning and shining light.

Jeremiah 20:9 And I can't stop: for if I say I will never again mention the Lord, never more speak in His name, then his words in my heart is like fire that burns in my bones and I can't hold it in any longer.

Your desire should always be to function in the revelation of the greater truth. Studying the life of our Lord Jesus will show you clearly how to walk in the greater reality of God's word.

Isaiah 33:24 and the inhabitants will not say "I am sick" The people who dwell in it will be forgiven their iniquity".

Divine healing is a truth and blessing from God. It is wonderful to know that no matter the nature of the sickness, you can receive healing. But there is a greater truth to that, and it is the fact that you can live in divine health everyday of your life.

I am talking about a state where you are sickness, diseases, and infirmity free, never needing to be healed. You never read in the bible that one day, Jesus had a cold or headache or contracted the flu and then sent Peter to assemble the other disciples to pray for Him to be healed. He was in control and always acted dominion. He lived health.

3 John 2 Beloved, I pray that you may prosper in all things and be in health just as your soul prospers.

Matthew 15.26 But he answered and said "it is not good to take the children's bread and throw it to the dogs.

Note that the Bible refers to healing as the ` children's bread. In order words, it is children (spiritual babes) that require healing or people who were ignorant of their identities. As you mature in the things of the Spirit, you leave the good things for the best, you move from asking for healing to living in divine health. This is the greater truth and the revelation by which you ought to live every day.

Proverbs 24:14 so shall the knowledge of wisdom be to you soul. If you have found it, there is a prospect. And your hope will not be cut off.

For you to receive your miracle and walk-in greater lights, you must be connected to the maker of miracle and giver of greater lights. Authority has been given, don't use the authority and leave the source behind. You must take both with you to be able to walk in greater lights in or be a testimony to God's glory.

Isaiah 29:13 Therefore the Lord said "Inasmuch as these people draw near with their mouths. And honor me with their lips. But have removed their hearts far from Me and their fear towards Me is taught by the commandments of men.

Acts 3:16 and His name, through faith in His name, has made this strong, whom you see and know. Yes the faith which comes through Him has given him his perfect soundness in the presence of you all.

God doesn't want good things to happen to you by chance only. He wants to do good things. He doesn't want tomorrow to come to you by surprise, when you declare tomorrow you will walk in the victory of Christ. You can create good things; they don't just happen. That's why the scriptures say in *1 John 4:4 "Greater is He who lives in you than he who lives in the world" and that whatsoever that overcomes the world is born of God and that in all these things you are more than a conqueror.* God wants tomorrow to be the fruits of your works today. Good things don't just happen; you make good things to happen.

Ephesians 1:11 In Him we have obtained an inheritance being predestined according to the purpose of Him who works all things according to the counsel of His will.

So, put the Word to work in your life, for the Word is the true light. Measure your life experiences with the word and the life of the Lord Jesus and function continually in the greater truths of the word. *John 16:13 However when the Spirit of truth has come, He will guide you into all truth, for He will not speak on His own authority but whatever He hears He will speak and He will tell you things to come.*